Fly Fishing for Beginners

GW00692102

By the same author
Mr Hundred Per Cent
Angling in New Zealand
Trout Flies In New Zealand
Tie a Fly
Nymphs for all Seasons
Boy Fisherman
Duckfever

Fly Fishing for Beginners

Keith Draper

REED

First published 1985
Reprinted 1987, 1989, 1991, 1993

Published by Reed Books,
a division of Octopus Publishing Group (NZ) Ltd,
39 Rawene Road, Birkenhead, Auckland. Associated
companies, branches and representatives throughout
the world.

This book is copyright. Except for the purpose of fair
reviewing, no part of this publication may be
reproduced or transmitted in any form or by any
means, electronic or mechanical, including
photocopying, recording, or any information storage
and retrieval system, without permission in writing
from the publisher. Infringers of copyright render
themselves liable to prosecution.

ISBN 0 7900 0084 9

Typeset by Typemakers International Ltd
Printed by Wing King Tong Co Ltd, Hong Kong

Dedication

For Mum, who years ago spent so many anxious evenings awaiting my return from the river while I, spellbound, full of boyish enthusiasm and oblivious of her concern, made countless "last casts" until the darkness sent me trudging home across the paddocks.

Acknowledgements

A book of this type just has to have good illustrations and Don Weller's drawings show very plainly the basics of fly casting.

John Parsons' fine photography beautifully illustrates the intricacies of the various ways of retrieving a fly line and the cover photo has the stamp of Parsons upon it. John, young Brendan Lewis and I spent a delightful afternoon together: Brendan and I fished while John busied himself with his camera, then he took up his rod and we fished together. Even the trout co-operated.

My poor publisher, Paul Bradwell, waited for this book far too long. It was a protracted birth and the most difficult thing I have ever written. You have no idea how difficult it is explaining the obvious — I hope I have done it justice.

My editor Graham Wiremu was very helpful. Here was an editor who was also an angler and brought another viewpoint to the scene.

Margaret will be pleased to read this. "When are you going to finish that — book?" she would ask with considerable emphasis. She didn't enjoy seeing all her typing languish.

Well here it is at last. I hope it will assist and encourage those who are drawn to the wonderful sport of fly fishing.

Keith Draper
Taupo, 1984

Contents

The moment of deception   1
1. The fly line   6
2. The fly rod 14
3. The fly reel 22
4. Leaders 26
5. Knots 29
6. Flies 37
7. Casting and retrieving 47
8. Fishing tactics 72
9. Fly fishing from a boat 86
10. After dark 88
11. Netting or beaching a fish 90
12. Wading 95
13. Aids and accessories 98
14. Handling the catch 101

Conclusion 103

This book has been written purely for beginners and I have deliberately sketched out only the bare bones of the sport. To do the subject full justice would take volumes. Once you have reached the stage where you have an understanding of the basics you are better equipped to read the hundreds of books and magazines which are dedicated to the subject. It takes time. There is no recipe for an instant fly fisher.

So this book is intended as a sort of watering can that produces the initial nourishment to assist the sprouting of the seed. Streamside experience and the assistance of other authors will serve to enrich its further growth.

The moment of deception

Fly fishing has fascinated some people since the earliest times. We have come a long way since our forebears used lines of plaited horsehair and 20-foot rods with tips of whalebone. Modern tackle developments have progressed beyond the wildest dreams of trout fishers of the middle ages, but the fascination has remained the same ever since the first fish was caught on a hook.

Fly fishing for trout, salmon and, to a growing extent, some of the sporting seafish species is the ultra refinement of angling sport. In fly fishing, the hook is craftily dressed with a mixture of fur, feather, tinsel and other materials to look like something worth eating or attacking — an insect or a small fish. It has to look as natural as possible in or on the water so we cannot use floats or weights or most of the paraphernalia associated with other forms of fishing. Accordingly special lines have been developed to enable you to reach your fish with the fly, and special rods are used to cast the lines. These are described in detail on the following pages, along with the techniques we use to make the most of our tackle. Modern fly-fishing tackle enables an angler to stalk the elusive quarry from a distance. With care and skill the fly can be presented in such a way that the most timid of fish will be fooled into taking it.

That is what fly fishing is all about — the deceiving of a fish, and to many fly anglers the "rise" or take of an artificial fly is the only true reward they seek. When you think about it, regardless of how exciting the battle may have been, or whether the fish was kept or released, the most important phase of the whole operation was when the fish actually took the fly — "the moment of deception". If that moment of deception never took place then the whole exercise would be in vain. The thrilling runs and leaps of a struggling trout through tumbled rapids and swift glides, and the final exultant moment as a spotted beauty is netted or beached, would never be known.

The types of people who indulge in fly fishing are many and they come from all walks of life.

Some take a very simple and realistic view of it as a sport to be enjoyed in all ways. They count their blessings every time they feel fresh mountain air flooding their lungs. Their nostrils fill with an aroma compounded of water, moss, bankside herbs, fresh foliage, wild flowers and the damp smell of forest mulch. They thrill to the sight of a rare bird, they wonder at the mystery of a mayfly hatch and their hearts jump at the splashy rise of a trout snatching a drifting insect from the surface of the tumbled clearwater stream. Their fingers fumble as they tie on a fresh fly in haste, always — but always — anticipating that perhaps this pattern will prove to be totally

The trout of our dreams: the tele-photo lens captures a giant brown trout lying in a stream. Estimated to weigh close to 10 kg (20 lb), this is the kind of fish anglers dream of catching — but such fish are wary and difficult to catch.

irresistible to every trout in the stream or lake.

Then there is the type of angler for whom every facet of the sport becomes a challenge to be finally unravelled, explained, and the scientific distillation of the knowledge applied in a more rational and expert way than has ever before been imagined.

There is too the type of angler for whom the cast is nothing more than the *coup de grâce*. The study and observation of the quarry are only the prelude to the cast — considered and schemed for several minutes before it is eventually made.

I once went fishing with an elderly gentleman who sat beside his favourite pool for nearly two hours one evening. His dry fly was carefully oiled after being tied to a very fine leader but it never drifted upon the surface of the pool that evening. It was early in the season and he never saw a single rise so he wasn't interested in making a cast. I dashed round the rest of the stream in youthful enthusiasm and was very proud of the two trout I had to show for my efforts. I couldn't understand the old angler's attitude at the time . . . I still don't but I'm beginning to.

So fly fishing is many things to many people. It has fascinated me ever since I can remember and many of my fishing friends are the same — we began by fishing for tiddlers in little streams and creeks. Some of us were born to be fishermen and were fortunate enough to be able to indulge our passion from an early age. Others have not been so lucky and have had to wait for opportunity to favour them.

I recently had among one of my fly-fishing classes a pupil who had turned seventy. He brought with him a complete set of brand-new fly-fishing gear which was forty years old. That many years before he had bought a dairy farm which bordered a trout stream so he thought that he would spend his spare time trout fishing. Unfortunately his farming duties proved to be so many, and so demanding, that he wasn't ready to fish until he sold his farm and retired. Others begin their fly fishing at an early age, and a child of twelve or so learns to fish very quickly.

The following pages summarise the teachings of my fly-fishing schools. You can never learn truly from a book. What you can do, though, is to combine reading with personal experience. When

3

A bag of rainbows: these lake fish were taken on a streamer fly, tied and fished to imitate the small fry and minnows on which they were feeding.

The brown trout: a real prize and a difficult fish to fool. When you've mastered the art of careful casting and delicate presentation you'll begin to catch brownies.

you have problems with some particular aspect of your fishing, consult the book and see where you are going wrong.

Most fly anglers have problems with their casting and I will state now what these problems are — I will be re-stating these throughout the book and I will emphasise them at the conclusion, and yet I know now that many of my readers will continue to ignore them. *You* determine to be one of the readers who won't. I don't care how much casting experience you may have had, remember these cardinal points now. Then ask yourself: am I observing them?

These points are:
1. Apply plenty of power to the rod (it's a propulsion tool, not a fairy godmother's wand).
2. Never drop the rod tip below its highest point during a back cast.
3. If you never make a good straight back cast you'll never make a good forward cast.

Remember these points. If you don't I'll be reminding you in the pages ahead. Of the three, the last is the most important — it has to be because it is the sum total of the two previous ones. Now read them again please. Having done that, we're going to consider the most important part of your equipment.

1. The fly line

People think the fly rod is the most important part of a fly fisher's tackle. Make no mistake — it is important, and is usually the most expensive piece of all equipment, but those who know will tell you that the single most important part of any fly fisher's tackle is the fly line.

You will be relying on your line to present your fly where the fish are (or where you think they are). It must be of the right weight and shape to enable you to cast the necessary distance; it must be of a certain density to reach the fish at the right level in the water; and in most circumstances it must perform these tasks as unobtrusively as possible.

Beginners will go into a shop with a fair idea of what they are prepared to spend. They usually look over the rods and reels, add together the prices of their preferences and then decide to settle for a cheap fly line because the rod and the reel have used up most of their budget. They

would be best advised to buy the most expensive line they can afford and if necessary cut back on the price of the reel. Some very adequate reels can be bought for reasonable prices. If you are not concerned with budgets and you're prepared to pay out $300 to $400 then by all means buy the best of everything. You are a fortunate person and don't need my advice except that I can only confirm that in fly fishing, as in all other walks of life, the very best does not come cheap. But to drive the point home once again for the angler on a budget (and most of us are): don't economise on your fly line.

Let's discuss fly lines. They come in a variety of colours, thicknesses and weights, and to a beginner they are very complex. To a shop assistant looking for a certain brand in size, engineering and specific gravity they can also seem to be complex. But they are basically divided into two groups — those which float and

Fly lines

Fly lines come in a variety of sizes, profiles and densities. Cheap lines may appeal to the budget-minded, but in the long run the more expensive will prove to be the best. Many cheap lines are very stiff and difficult to handle, and frequently the plastic coating doesn't last long. Lines with cracked coatings are difficult to cast.

If properly equipped, you'll need at least three lines: a floater, a slow sinker and a fast sinker. With these you're ready for most situations.

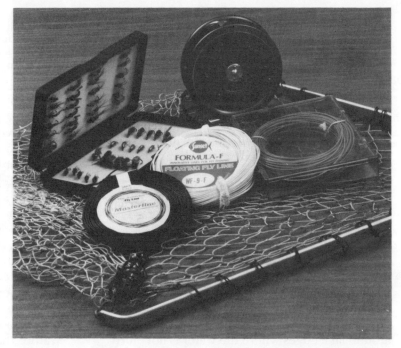

those which sink.

Floaters are obvious — they literally float on the surface of the water. They are constructed in such a way that their specific gravity is less than that of water and unless they are soiled with grime they should remain on the surface except perhaps during use in very rough and tumbled water when the sheer violence of the water's surface may drive them under. But they are nevertheless floating

7

lines and are all designated by the letter F wherever you see the line code printed on the box label. They usually come in light colours so that fish cannot see them so easily against the sky — yet the angler can see them easily enough to follow their progress on the water.

Sinkers come into several groups which may be distinguished as slow sinkers, medium sinkers, fast sinkers and superfast sinkers. Different manufacturing companies have their own codes for designating each group. There are times when each line has its own particular merit.

A *slow-sinking line* is used for fishing lake edges where only a moderate depth is required and the use of a faster sinking line would tangle your fly in weed beds or snag it among rocks.

A *medium-sinking line* is fine on moderately deep and slower-flowing streams and for fishing around lake edges where the water is not more than about two meters deep.

A *fast-sinking line* is ideal for fast rivers with deep holes and for fishing off ledges into lakes.

A *superfast sinker* is fairly restricting unless you really want to be scratching bottom all the time

and losing a lot of flies. It's really best suited for only the biggest of rivers and deep holes and drop-offs in lakes.

You'll usually find the range of sinking lines in dark colours like dark green or brown, to merge in with the general colour scheme of the bottom. That gives us a coverage of all the types of line densities you're liable to find on the shelf of the tackle store — but that's only the beginning of it.

Floaters, slow sinkers, medium sinkers, fast sinkers and superfast sinkers are all determined by their specific gravity rather than by their actual weight. Lines are also graded according to their weight, and for most purposes you will be using lines numbering from 5 or 6 at the lighter end of the scale up to 9 or 10 at the heaviest. Rods and lines should be used in a balanced combination, so if you use a No. 6 line your rod should be marked No. 6 too. Why you should choose one weight rather than another is explained later.

Then as well as these classifications you will also find the following list of line profiles.

Level: floating and sinking
Double-taper: floating and sinking
Weight-forward: floating and sinking

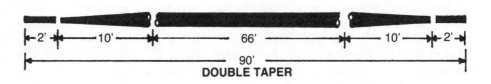

75'
LEVEL

The basic shapes of fly lines
The measurements, which are in imperial feet, give the key to the true proportions of each line type. Some manufacturers vary these proportions, especially in the weight-forward style. Some make the business end of the taper longer than usual so that it can be used for finer work on a short line, enabling you to use a weight-forward line even for delicate presentation of your fly at short range. But you still have the advantage of the fine shooting diameter at the rear end of the line to assist long-distance casting when required.

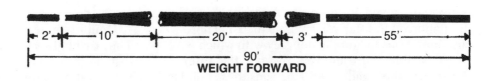

2' — **10'** — **66'** — **10'** — **2'**
90'
DOUBLE TAPER

2' — **10'** — **20'** — **3'** — **55'**
90'
WEIGHT FORWARD

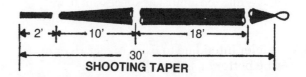

2' — **10'** — **18'**
30'
SHOOTING TAPER

9

Shooting-taper: floating and sinking

Sink-tip: a combination, being a weight-forward floater with a sinking tip.

Why on earth do we have all these types to complicate things further? Let's deal with them one at a time, because there really is a use for each one of them.

Level lines are just that — 25 m of parallel line. They come off the machine in a continuous length and are just chopped off at regular intervals, rolled up and packaged. It's a simple operation and these lines are the cheapest and in many ways very satisfactory if you are prepared to accept a limitation on how far you are able to cast. There are limitations too on the delicacy with which you'll be able to present your fly upon the water. In some of the smaller faster streams these points may not matter and an angler — especially if on a tight budget — may be almost as successful using a level line as with the obvious choice — a double taper.

But the angler intending to fish a bigger river or lake would be better off using a line offering greater distance (a weight-forward or a shooting taper). Or if the stream is very clear with smooth glides then the lighter end of a tapered fly line would enable the presentation of a fly with less disturbance to the surface of the water. In some streams populated with shy, educated trout, this is a very important factor.

So the level line, while it could be used in all situations, is really a second-best. The level line is fly fishing's jack-of-all-trades — but master of none.

Conclusion: a fine line for beginners with limited funds and more particularly suited to wet-fly fishing on smaller rough streams.

Double-taper lines are the universal fly line. They cast better than a level, adding to your distance as well as enabling a more gentle presentation. They certainly won't cast as far as weight-forward lines or shooting tapers, but with one of these you can cast 20 or 30 m under favourable conditions, which is plenty of distance in most circumstances. If I was allowed only one type of fly line, this style would be my choice if only for the fact that a more careful presentation of the fly is possible, especially when dry-fly fishing, and of course a double-tapered line is reversible should the forward end become worn.

Conclusion: a good all-round line which forms the basis of a fly fisher's line requirements.

Weight-forward (rocket-taper or torpedo) lines were designed for one basic purpose — to achieve greater distance. They are all built the same way and are ideal for achieving an extra six metres or more on big water. The finer diameter of the rear or reel end of the line — which we call the "shooting line" — creates less friction, offers less air and weight resistance, and "follows through" after the final delivery punch of the rod has been made.

However, if not carefully retrieved and coiled, it is very prone to looping over itself and forming a snarl which jams in the butt guide of the rod. This liability is compounded when fishing in the dark and I've often had occasions with a hooked trout on the end of the fly line and a snarled tangle of retrieved shooting line.

A specialised form of the weight-forward line is the bug taper, which has a very short forward-tapered section which improves the "turn-over" of a large fly at the completion of a cast so that the fly lands out ahead of the line and doesn't collapse in a heap on top of it. To a certain extent this same effect can be achieved by cutting off some of the taper of a regular weight-forward line so that the taper is reduced to a couple of metres.

I like weight-forward lines — almost as much as double-tapered. I like them for nymphing and dry-fly fishing on the bigger waters and of course for still-water fishing or wading the mouth of a stream they are always first choice except that when fishing after dark a double-taper causes less trouble from snarled loops when shooting the retrieved line. In this situation the distance that can be achieved by the use of a weight-forward line has to be sacrificed in return for more trouble-free casting. But even in the dark, when fish are hanging far out in the lake or drifting off the end of the dying current from a stream mouth, distance must be achieved even at the risk of occasional tangles.

Weight-forwards are at their best in daylight when you can keep your eye on your coiling or knitting during retrieve (see pp. 62-6). They are not suited to super-careful presentation but on the faster, rougher type of stream they make good nymphing lines and can be used for dry-fly fishing as well. With a fast-sinking weight-forward the finer diameter of the shooting line causes less resistance against the flow of the river and allows the head to fish more deeply than would be possible with a double-taper or level line.

Conclusion: weight-forward lines are designed primarily for casting long distances but over short distances they do not perform quite as well as double-tapers.

The shooting taper (or shooting head) is a short fly line of about 10 m which is attached to a very light shooting or running line. It is really an advanced form of the weight-forward line. The short heavy section of fly line is aerialised and then when the delivery cast is made the very light running line is drawn through the guides with a minimum of effort, allowing very long casts to be made. The running line may be one of several types. Some use a monofilament nylon of a fairly limp type which has less tendency to hang in tight spring-like coils. Then there is a flat monofilament

nylon available which is very popular. Another type is a floating running line which is in reality nothing other than a very fine floating fly line.

I do come across some anglers using shooting heads where, because of the restricted size of the water, they don't need them and would be better off using either a double-taper or a weight-forward line. However, where depth must be achieved in fast or heavy water, the fine diameter of the running line does allow a high-density shooting head to sink more deeply as it presents less resistance against the flow of the river.

Conclusion: shooting tapers are really only necessary if you need to make really long casts, which under normal fishing conditions would be in excess of 30 m. If the type of fishing dictates very long casts, this is the style of fly line to use. However, perseverance will be necessary before full control of the shooting line is achieved.

The sink tip is a compromise line, and while some may argue that there is a case for its use, it does very little that can't be done with other styles of line.

It is basically a weight-forward floating line, the

taper of which is dressed with a heavy plastic causing it to sink at the business end. One of its benefits is that it is easier to pick up off the water when beginning a new cast. One of the claims made for it is that it is "ideal for wet-fly and nymph fishing when fish are at a depth beyond the range of a floating line". Why not use a medium sinker then, I ask. However, to be fair, I have used one in lakes around medium-depth stream mouths with considerable success.

Conclusion: a specialist line with restricted use.

Care of the line

The modern fly line is made of hard-wearing plastic and needs minimal care. Gone, thankfully, are the days when lines were made of silk and had to be oiled to float and then dried carefully after fishing trips to avoid rot and mildew.

However, certain common-sense measures should be taken with your expensive fly line. Be careful when putting your rod down on a sandy or gravelly bank. Grit may get into the reel, damaging not only the reel but abrading the surface of the line too. Worn rod guides will also scratch the line. They should be checked regularly for wear and replaced if necessary.

When taking the spool out of the cage of the reel and putting it back again, take care that the line is not nipped between the two. Most spools have a notch cut into the side through which the line can pass to avoid being pinched.

Keep an eye on the ends of your line. Through wear and tear cracks may appear. After a while these may influence the ability of a floating line to float properly. With a double-taper line you can always simply reverse the line, and with any line it will do no harm to cut off a few centimetres. Check the knots you've used to tie your line to the backing and to the leader. Over a period you may find that these have bitten into the plastic coating of the line so much that you need to cut off the knot and tie them again.

Floating lines need cleaning occasionally and wiping with silicone grease, which is readily available from sports stores.

Following these simple precautions you will find that your line serves you well for years.

2. The fly rod

A rod that may be one person's dream could well prove to be another's curse. Some anglers will fish with any old rod at all and perform well — others will be in continual search of a new rod as they become disenchanted with their latest acquisition.

Various factors should influence your decision when you buy a fly rod. An obvious one is whether you can afford it, and this will depend largely on the materials from which it is constructed. But other considerations are just as important if you are to make the most of your fishing. A rod's length, weight and action, adding up to the "feel" of the rod, need to be borne in mind — not only with regard to the kind of fishing you want to do but to your own physique.

A rod must feel right. It must be in harmony with the line (see p. 8) and be balanced with a reel that is neither too light nor too heavy. A large person can use a heavier, more powerful rod than can a smaller person. Because of greater physical strength, the large person — all other things being equal — should be able to cast further than those of lesser physique. Those of moderate build should use a rod to match their size. Let the big guy cast a country mile — it doesn't mean he'll catch more fish except in special circumstances. Right now I want to help the small guy's confidence.

Most streams and rivers seldom require a cast much in excess of 20 m. A cast much longer than that would land well up into the bushes on the far side. So what use are 40 m casts on such water? On big, wide rivers long casts are a definite advantage, but we don't all fish rivers of that type very often. Long casts are also necessary on lakes where fish lie right out where the dying current of a stream becomes one with the lake. But there are many small and medium streams which draw fish into the closer margins of the lake.

Stillwater fishing on lakes can be very

Fly rods and reels

There's an outfit to suit every pocket.

The rod on the left is a low-priced fibre-glass rod with a popular Japanese reel. While priced to meet the beginner's market it is in no way below standard.

Second from left is a better-quality fibre-glass rod with a Berkley fly reel. The finish of the rod is better. Higher quality fittings and rings have been used.

Third from left is a graphite rod with a Sage reel. This is a powerful rod designed for big water and heavy fish. The rod costs twice as much as a fibre-glass one but the extra power comes along with a lighter rod.

The last rod is made of Boron — a further development from the graphite range costing half as much again. This rod is complemented with a Shimano Bantam reel, an exquisite piece of engineering.

The finer, more expensive, rods will not make experts out of learners, but once the art of fly casting has been fully mastered, the extra performance they can deliver will be fully appreciated.

Rods illustrated are from the Wynrod range of quality tackle.

frustrating, and the trout gulping down hatching sedge or midges under your very rod tip, or smashing among bait fish herded along the lake margins, are not going to be impressed in the least by great rolling loops of line which present the fly metres out past the weed beds.

So a moderate cast will, for most of the time, prove to be quite sufficient and on those other occasions just do your best and have the grace to admire the casting of someone who can really reach out to the unreachable places. Better to cast 20 m regularly with ease than achieve 30 at the expense of exhausting or exasperating yourself.

Brute strength isn't the last word in casting skill, of course, and later on we'll be showing you techniques to achieve extra distance. Nevertheless, if you're fishing all day those extra few grams of a heavier rod casting a heavier line begin to tell. Wrist, arm and shoulder get tired and your performance suffers. So buy the lightest rod you can afford for the kind of fishing you propose to do.

How long? Very long rods are only used in specialist situations. The most popular lengths are between 2.4 and 2.8 m (8 ft-9 ft 6 in) and you will probably find the rod of your choice within this range. Remember that if you are going to be engaged in upstream dry-fly or nymph work you will be better off with a lighter rod than if you are fishing downstream with a wet-fly or streamer.

Upstream fishing is a very busy form of fly casting where at least four times as many casts are made as when downstream fishing, so the weight of the rod becomes of vital importance. This style of fishing — if carried out with a heavy rod — can be crippling, yet the same rod could be employed all day when used for downstream fishing with no ill effects being felt at all.

So if your fishing is to be of the type where you are going to be using large wet and streamer flies and fishing for large trout, then obviously a stouter rod is called for — probably one to take a No. 8 line or even a No. 9 or 10.

If you are going to be nymphing or dry-fly fishing — or even upstream wet-fly fishing, then a lighter rod handling a No. 6 or 7 line should be your choice.

If smallish trout and ultralight tackle are your choice, then you will be looking for a small rod perhaps anything from 1.8 to 2.3 m (6 ft-7 ft 6 in) and handling a No. 4 or 5 line, although these weights seem to be the choice of experienced specialists rather than beginners.

A fly rod needs a stiffer butt action with a quick tip if it is to be used for dry-fly fishing and also, I believe, upstream nymphing — although a softer type of rod will often do the latter quite well. For wet-fly and streamer fishing a more supple rod is desired, but don't confuse supple with soft or sloppy. The reasons for this will be dealt with later in greater detail but roll-casting can play an important part in nymph and wet-fly fishing so a rod having less tip action is suited — although if the rod is to be used for both dry-fly and nymph, pick the stiffer rod.

So having arrived at the rod rack in your sports store, what other criteria should we consider? Rods are manufactured from a variety of materials these days, each with its own characteristics and its own price. Let's consider them.

Carbon-fibre rods — or graphite rods as they are also called — are by far the best for modern fly fishing. They are also the most expensive but if you can stretch to affording it buy one and you'll never regret it. They do not make expert anglers out of tyros, just through virtue of what they are, but they help by making fishing much easier — because of their lightness and speedy tip recovery. They have less vibration than rods made from other materials.

Hollow fibre-glass rods are still the biggest sellers and are available in a much lower price bracket. Some of the cheaper glass fly rods are in fact very good value and often incorporate a blank exactly the same as one used in more expensive rods. To achieve a lower price, shortcuts are made on the fittings and finish of the rod. I know several anglers who have been using such rods for years. Some of them improve their performance by removing the line guides, repositioning them with the addition of another couple and binding them back on. Several coats of varnish carefully applied greatly boost the final appearance of the rod, which is then usually good for many years of service.

The cheaper rods usually have metal ferrules and with much wear these tend to work loose. Much more satisfactory is the glass-to-glass joint.

17

This may take the form of either a spigot or a sleeve ferrule. In both cases the fit is engineered to allow for wearing on. The use of a little candle wax rubbed onto the male joint also helps to keep the rod firmly jointed. This waxing should be done every now and then as a regular precaution to prevent your rod tip from flying out into the river in mid-cast.

Split-cane rods are pretty much a thing of the past except that there is still a small band of selective anglers around the world who believe that nothing surpasses a good-quality split-cane — or split-bamboo — rod. I might stress that they are not all doddery old-timers hooked on nostalgia either. Some of them are leaders in the field of angling. Split-cane rods are still made by some of the world's leading tackle companies for discerning fly fishers who do not mind paying a lot of money for a beautiful piece of crafted excellence. I often handle these exquisite rods and when I think of some of the rough situations I get myself into when fishing, I realise they are not for me. It would be sacrilege to drag them through brambles and bracken on the way to ambuscade

trout in a forest-locked pool. If, however, my fishing was restricted to open pastoral streams with manicured margins, pride of ownership and sheer appreciation of the workmanship of a beautiful angling tool would probably prompt me to invest in one of these modern echoes of a past age.

I do have split-cane rods in my possession but they were built to the standard of split-cane rods as they used to be 40 or more years ago when a 7- or 8-ounce rod (200-225 g) was considered moderately light. The modern cane rods are slender wispy things, only a fraction of the weight of their predecessors. Modern glues combined with resin impregnation of the cane cells have made this possible. Cane is a natural product and, as with many things, there are those who will always believe that natural fibres are best.

When you're choosing a rod, therefore, remember that price need not be a criterion of what is best suited for your purposes. To a very large extent you get only what you pay for — sometimes expressed in more expensive fittings and greater care and finish before the rod is ready for sale. Some of the "name" rods may be more expensive but they are always a good buy because the companies that make them are prepared to stand by their products and will guarantee them against all defects — something you certainly can't expect from a cheaper rod.

If you live on the water a one-piece rod is ideal for you. The only trouble is that rods have to be transported and so the necessity for rods of two- or three-piece construction arises. Two-piece are by far the most popular. If ever trouble is experienced with a rod it is almost always with the ferrules, so the fewer the rod has, the less probability of any trouble.

Today we nearly all have our own transport, and cars and stationwagons have ample room to carry a two-piece rod. Occasionally an angler will have reasons for needing a three-piece rod. Perhaps you ride a bike or want to hike into remote fishing places — in which case you will be looking for a four-piece or even five-piece rod.

Certainly if you do a lot of air travel or spend much of your summer exploring remote mountain streams on foot, where several hours of hiking from the road is required, then a multiple breakdown rod is ideal, but it will seldom do the job as well as a nicely balanced two-piece rod. The extra joints affect the response of the rod and can actually deaden much of the action, but when you have to push through miles of rough country or manage a long rod case through airlines, then you're prepared to put up with these minor drawbacks. In such cases rods which fit into a suitcase or a backpack are a boon rather than a burden. Otherwise avoid them: the more sections there are to a rod the more likelihood of trouble. The same can be said of telescopic rods.

Occasionally you will see two-handled fly rods, with a second small handle, known as a fighting butt, beneath the reel fitting. Although a few old-timers still use them for big trout, their use these days is more often limited to salmon and some sea species. They are very much specialist tools, and throughout this book we will be assuming that you are using the more orthodox single-handed rod.

Care of the rod

Cheaper rods come in a polythene sleeve or nothing at all. The better ones are supplied with a cloth rod bag sewn into divided compartments, while the more expensive models are usually supplied with a protective carrying tube as well — usually aluminium or hard polypropylene.

For storing, split-cane rods need to be looked after carefully. Don't keep them in the carrying case during periods of use. Make sure they are dry and then hung in their cloth bags.

Glass rods can take a fair bit of knocking around. I have seen some which are actually neglected and yet they continue to perform. First things to suffer are the guide bindings. These bindings can become scuffed with use and need to be checked once in a while and given a protective coat of clear polyurethane varnish to prevent further wear. This will prevent one of the binding threads from breaking through and hanging loose.

Keep an eye on the condition of the guides. Worn line-guides develop little grooves and sharp edges and these can play havoc with expensive fly lines. Once a line guide shows any sign of wear, replace it and check all the others at the same time, as usually wear on one means that the rest are close to becoming unusable as well.

Cork has long remained the favourite of fly anglers for their rod grips, and I am no exception.

I guess it's tradition more than any other reason. I have seen rods with grips of preformed plastic and of course there is the new hyperlon which feels good — but doesn't look right. I certainly know that given the choice of cork or some of the newer plastic type materials, nearly all customers prefer cork.

However cork deteriorates with use and it will eventually crumble if not looked after. Please don't use the grip to impale your fly during those times you are walking along the bank. Use the little keeper ring or loop which is mounted on the stem of some rods just in front of the grip. Or hook it on to one of the pillars of the reel. But please don't stick it into the cork of the grip. Keep the grip clean — a wash with soapy water does wonders and should be done at least at the end of each season.

If the cork is beginning to show signs of wear it can be strengthened by varnishing. This soaks in and makes the surface more resilient but it doesn't really help the look. The grip nearly always wears just where you apply pressure with your thumb. This can be overcome by taping around this spot with modern insulating tape.

If your rod has metal ferrules do not leave it jointed together for any length of time, as the ferrules often become stuck and to remove them can be difficult. Glass-to-glass joints don't have these problems except that if they have been treated with too much wax on the spigot they can become cemented together during cold weather. The judicious application of a little heat will usually remedy this and I have even overcome it by holding the joint in my hand for several minutes. My body temperature was enough to soften the wax and allow the rod to be dismantled.

Here the angler ties a fly to his tapered leader. The rod, an 8-footer (2.4 m) is an ideal length for smaller streams.

3. The fly reel

Fly reels have long held a fascination over anglers. If you have one on your table and a fisherman comes in, in all likelihood he'll pick it up and begin revolving the drum, listening to the clicking sound of the pawl being sprung by the sprocket. That same click sets up a shrill song of delight when a hooked trout quarters the swift flow of a river in a wild bid for freedom. It's a sound to thrill any angler.

I have a collection of reels — some old ones of brass or wood, others of a later date but still of ancient lineage — and they all progress to the modern fly reel, a beautiful piece of engineering based on a long history in search of angling perfection.

Reels range from the very cheap and near-useless to expensive, beautiful creations which are a joy to behold. But the truth is reels are a very personal thing and what really matters is that they store line when not being used and give and withdraw line in the actual practice of casting or playing a fish. This is the basis upon which a reel should be judged, and there are many reels of moderate price available which do just that.

The majority of fly reels on world markets today originate in Asian factories — some of them blatant copies of well-known models from long-respected tackle houses.

Some of these reels are "ships spoiled for a hap'orth of tar" and I can think of several models which, for the expenditure of a few more cents on original production, would be quite serviceable reels. But others are of excellent value and will stand up to years of service. If you aspire to a Hardy, be prepared to pay a lot more, remembering that there will always be a price for excellence. For obvious reasons I cannot name reels which fall short of the required standards, but the following are points to watch for.

Is the reel a serviced model — can you buy spare spools and parts for it? If you can, you may assure yourself that it is a reel that intends to be around for a while.

Check the spool for sloppiness and ensure there is no great tolerance between the edge of the spool and the reel cage. Is the spool easily removed for bankside changing or cleaning? Is the handle a good size and firmly attached to the plate of the spool? Is the ratchet system sound and the spring a good one and not merely a piece of pressed metal?

Is it large enough to carry sufficient line for the type of fishing you will be using it for? Now that's a good question so we'd better go into it in more detail.

Normally, for most fishing except for the biggest of trout, a regular fly line of 30 m with 50 m of backing is perfectly adequate, so you must have a reel which will carry this amount of line at least. If you are fishing a water renowned for its larger fish (and I'm thinking of trout up to and in excess of 4-5 kg) then you'll need at least another 50 m of backing. So choose a reel according to your needs. In practice, even with large trout you will seldom need more than 50 m of backing, but should you ever hook a really big fish, it pays to be prepared.

I can count on my fingers the number of times I have needed a full 100 metres.

One factor which must influence your decision on a reel is its weight. If you are using a light rod, you must use a reel to match. If you find this means a restricted line capacity the problem may be overcome in several ways. One is that if you fish small streams you can cut your double-taper fly line in half which gives you 15 m of casting line with room for the extra backing created by removing half of the bulk of the line. A further 20-30 m of backing can be fitted on to a reel if a weight-forward line instead of a double-taper is used. The diameter of the backing can be decreased allowing more to be fitted onto the reel provided the breaking strain isn't too low. As a general rule, if you use a backing about twice the breaking strain of your nylon, you can't go wrong.

Graphite has made its appearance on the reel market as well as that of the rod. My prize combination is an extra-light graphite reel on a graphite rod and the combination is one with which it is a delight to fish. This reel has taken some fairly hard knocks, including coming off the top of the car at more than 100 km per hour which left it with a couple of slight marks on it, but it survived the unwelcome test extremely well.

Care of the reel
Reels have a habit of collecting grains of sand and grit in their internal workings. The oil and grease on the spindle dry out if not replaced. A wipe with a rag and a brushing with petrol or a solvent do help, but if the line is still on the spool make sure you don't spill any of the cleaner on to it. Use grease to smear on the spindle — don't use a light oil such as is used for sewing machines. Once again, take care to keep it off the line.

Check all the screws — if it is the type of reel which has screws attaching the side plates to the rod pillars, remove them and dip them in lacquer or varnish or even glue before replacing them. Take special care with the screws attaching the foot to the frame. These come under a fair amount of stress with continual winding of the reel.

The precautions I have described will prevent the possibility of screws dropping out and your reel coming adrift when you're in the middle of playing trout.

Backing
Backing should not be confused with running or shooting line, which is attached to a short shooting head.

Backing is the reserve line carried on a reel behind the fly line so that should you hook a big strong fish which you cannot reasonably hold, then it is possible to allow it to run without danger of coming to the end of the line and suffering a break. We have already discussed this to some extent when dealing with reel capacities but let's decide exactly what we intend using for backing.

There are several types on the market, made of braided dacron or the like. This is usually 10 to 12 kg breaking strain which is an advisable strength but it is possible to go much lighter, especially if trying to gain extra yardage on a reel drum. But in doing this care must be used not to go too light. I would be very reluctant to go below 5 kg. Sometimes when a fish has run out all your fly line plus a good measure of backing, it happens that the fly line fouls around a submerged boulder and

Sometimes you need a fast pair of legs
Frank Draper in hot pursuit of a trout which was hooked well above white water in the photo. For most circumstances a 30 m fly line and 50 m of backing are adequate. However, in lakes and big rivers where large trout are likely to be encountered 100 m of backing is recommended.

this requires a tug-of-war to free it (sometimes at the expense of a good fish). So bear this in mind especially if you are fishing the larger types of waters. On medium to small streams it doesn't matter nearly so much.

I have used nylon monofilament for backing for years with no regrettable results. I've seen reels split their drums from the pressure of tightly wound mono but they weren't fly reels. We were bottom-fishing at sea and dragging half a kilo of lead plus two struggling fish up through water over 100 m deep puts a strain on the reel far in excess of what can ever be expected fly fishing a stream.

4. Leaders

Obviously you cannot tie a fine fly to the end of a thick conspicuous fly line. Between the line and the fly we use a length of nylon monofilament known as a leader (you will occasionally hear them called casts and traces too, but leader is the universally accepted term these days and it certainly avoids confusion).

Take my tip and use tapered leaders. They are much easier to cast with than level leaders because the rhythm and power of your cast continues on through the line and along the leader. Tapered leaders can be bought already nicely tapered from loop to point and they last for ages.

You buy a couple of tapered leaders which should last you most of the season, accidents barred, and a spool of 2 or 3 kg monofilament.

When the end of your leader begins to diminish due to break-offs and losing a few centimetres every time you change a fly, just blood-knot on another length — or tippet, as we call the end section. You can make the tippet a little longer than usual if you think it necessary. Suppose you decide that the trout are scaring too easily — perhaps you need a longer and lighter leader. Don't change it, just add another tippet of a lighter weight.

What length should your nylon be? For general all-round purposes, about 3 m is fine but there are times when you can go much shorter, especially in the dusk and after dark. Trout cruise into shallow places after dark searching for minnows and other forage foods. So a shortened leader used on a floating line enables you to keep your fly up off the bottom where it is liable to snag. It is possible to shorten your nylon to just half a metre or so without the trout seeming to become frightened. In these cases a length of level nylon is best used.

However, there are times when longer leaders are desirable, either because of very clear water conditions or when nymph fishing in deep water. At times like this it pays to go to leaders of 5 m or so.

How do you control such long leaders? Well it's hard in the face of a stiff breeze, or any sort of breeze for that matter, but provided the leader is tapered you have a fair measure of control over its performance while casting.

Where can you buy tapered leaders of 5 m? Frankly I don't know, and the way to extend your leader to this length is to add on to a regular 3 m leader. Normally if we want a bit of extra length to a leader, say increasing it to 4 m, we merely take a regular tapered leader a size or two heavier than the desired weight and add the extra length by way of a tippet. However, when you need to go to 5 m it is better to take a tapered leader of the tip size required and extend it by adding to the butt end. To do this you need a fairly heavy-gauge nylon — about 15 kg or so — but this heavy butt will give you a much better turnover of your nylon at the end of the cast.

A very long leader can be an asset in clear water conditions or when fishing for educated trout. I personally prefer this approach rather than going down to a very light line. If you are fishing with a relatively heavy fly outfit, say a No. 8, it is possible by using an extended leader to make casts with a minimum of disturbance but still retain a line heavy enough to buck breezes.

Wind is the curse of anglers everywhere and all waters receive their fair share of it, especially during the equinoctial periods. The heavier line enables you to overcome this to some degree and of course if the day turns out still and bright then you can go out to a longer leader.

Leaders should fall on the water fairly straight. If your leader is landing in a heap of springy coils, it needs straightening. Just pull it through a piece of rubber inner tube a few times and you'll be amazed at the difference it makes. I always carry a small square of it in my vest and on occasions when I can't find it I use the strap of my waders. You could rivet a piece of rubber onto your vest so that you don't lose it. Just fold the rubber over the nylon and draw through under tension.

What weight nylon should you use? To answer that we need to know what sort of fly fishing you will be doing because it depends on several things.

Trout feeding in placid or slow-flowing clear water on bright days, will be easily frightened off by nylon which is too heavy. Under such circumstances it is necessary to go fairly light and I call fairly light 1 to 1.5 kg. Anything under that is ultra-light.

I would call 1.5-2 kg tippets light; 2-3 kg standard; 3-4 kg stout; 5-6 kg heavy; 7-9 kg ultra heavy.

But your choice of leader weight may be influenced by several factors. What is the use of light leaders on water where you have to turn fish from snags or be broken nearly every time you hook a fish of some size? I know several such streams. They are full of smallish trout which rise beautifully to dry fly. But nearly every time I hook a fish of some size, and I mean of 1.5 kg upwards, the results are almost inevitable — especially with a light leader. However if you use too heavy a leader they often won't take your fly; it is better to use a heavier leader and take your chances.

But if you are fishing a stream with nice open gravelly pools and not too much heavy water then of course you can go lighter and let the fish have its way.

5. Knots

The knots you use are very important. Study the knots shown and learn them thoroughly. The waterside is not the place to begin learning by trial and error. Learn to tie your knots at home, then test them to destruction. Make sure your knots are good ones. It can be heartbreaking to have your holiday spoilt by losing the fish of a lifetime because of a poorly tied knot.

When tying nylon, moisten the knot with saliva before pulling tight. This lubricates the nylon and makes a nice snug knot pulled to the correct tension throughout.

You'll need to know knots for three purposes:

1 Tying loops to connect your fly line and nylon leader.

2 Joining lengths of nylon together.

3 Attaching flies to your leader.

The following are the knots I'm prepared to recommend to a beginner. There are dozens of variations, and even different ways to tie some of the ones shown, but my job is to keep things simple. So as you progress with your fly-fishing skills you will learn of the other knots and add some of them to your store. But the ones shown should suffice for the rest of your angling days; they have all been well tried and tested and will serve you well so long as you tie them with care.

The perfection loop

This knot is a hangover from the days of silkworm
gut. It ties a beautiful loop and is well worth
mastering. With a little practice you'll pick up the
knack of it but if you are one of those people who
have trouble understanding knots don't be
frightened to fall back on the blood bight knot for
making loops.

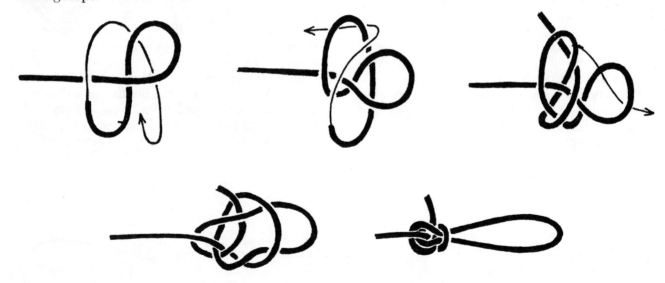

The blood bight knot

This knot is an excellent one for tying a loop at the end of your leader. Moisten it before pulling tight and snip off the unwanted end. It's quick and it's easy to remember, though the perfection loop is considered to be superior.

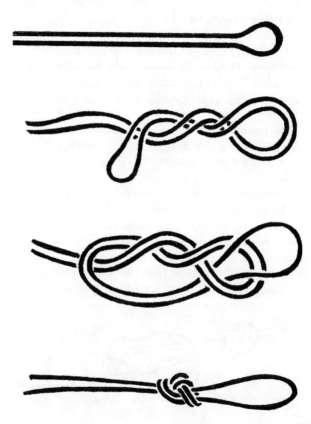

The tucked sheet bend

This knot is usually used only as an emergency but it's handy to know. In the illustration the black line represents the fly line and the loop the end of the nylon leader. It's quick and a rough and ready way of joining fly line and leader but it's very effective.

The problem with this join is that you have to take care that it doesn't jam in the top ring of the rod and it's a real certainty to jam if your rod has snake guides. So be warned, as in the excitement of landing a fish a beginner nearly always winds the fly line and leader join through the top guides.

However, if you have broken the end of your fly line off on a snag deep in the river it's a quick way to join on another leader. We haven't always the patience to sit down on the riverside trying to tie a nail knot when the trout are busily feeding.

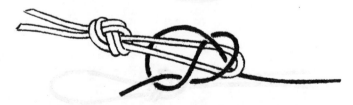

Nail or tube knot

This knot is used to attach the butt end of a leader to a fly line. In the illustration the fly line is the one on the left. As you can see a piece of small tubing is laid along the end of the fly line and the nylon is wrapped over both the tube and the line. After five turns the nylon is then inserted through the tube. The tube is slid off the end of the leader, then, holding the join between the finger and thumb of one hand, it is carefully pulled tight. I grip one end of the nylon in my teeth, and pull the other end with the free fingers of one hand, being careful to hold the join between the thumb and index finger of the other hand.

You may need to make several attempts before you get it right but when you do you'll find it results in a nice neat knot biting into the fly line. With some of the cheaper types of line this knot will bite through the skin of the dressing and slip off. If this happens you'll have to resort to looping the leader and line together.

For a tube, the centre of a ballpoint pen is excellent after it has been cleaned out. Of course you may use a nail, as the title suggests, and instead of having a tube to thread the nylon through you carefully thread the nylon between the nail and line, removing the nail when ready to pull the knot tight.

When out on the river and needing to tie a new knot, I have always found the ideal implement in the form of a piece of grass straw, broken off to the right length of about 10 cm or a pine needle which, with its natural groove, is an excellent tool to assist in the tying of this most useful knot. Trimmed off it passes through the rings of the rod with hardly any problems. Some give it a coating of plastic glue, tapered at both ends, to make it even more streamlined.

Another method which has stood the test is to open the end of the fly line by inserting a needle. The butt of the nylon, after careful cleaning, is treated with one of the new quick-setting high-power adhesives and inserted into the end of the fly line. This must be done very quickly.

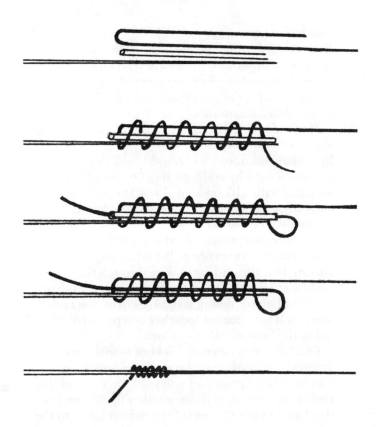

The blood knot

Every fly fisherman needs to know the blood knot. It's a very important one and tied properly it's strong. All knots reduce the given strength of any nylon but with the blood knot strength loss is reduced to a minimum.

If a leader is reduced in length because of a snag up, or snipping off a few centimetres every time a fly is changed, it can be brought back to its original length by adding a short tippet of nylon attached with a blood knot. Look at the illustration carefully and note that approximately four turns are made on either side. Make the crossed-over ends quite generous as short ones will make the knot difficult to execute in the latter stages. Ensure that the ends are taken through the middle at opposite sides from each other. Moisten the knot before pulling it tight. Snip off the ends and you'll have joined together two pieces of nylon the best way that's known.

Of course you can use this knot to make up a tapered leader of several connected lengths. If you want to fish two flies you may leave one of the ends long enough to tie on another fly. When I do this I always use the end of the nylon closest to the fly line as a dropper. The other end is snipped off, of course.

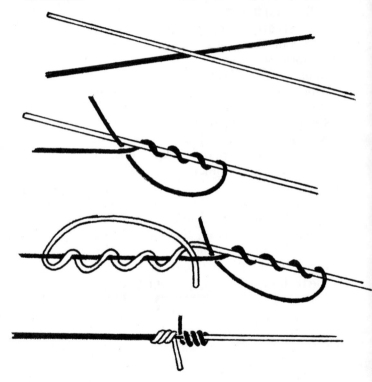

34

The half blood knot

This knot is also known as the clinch knot. It's simple and it's quick. It can be made even safer if the end of the nylon is brought back through the main loop. Moisten before pulling tight then trim off the excess.

This knot is particularly suited to tying on small flies, and especially dries, as it doesn't mess up the hackles of the fly. But if using larger flies such as lures tied on hooks 2-8 I recommend the turle knot.

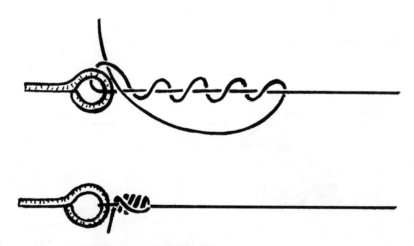

The turle knot

This knot is ideal to use with flies having upturned or downturned eyes. The illustration shows an upturned eye but exactly the same procedure is used for the downturned version. The advantage of this knot is that the fly will always swim straight and with streamer-type lures that's important, we think.

When you want to change flies this knot is easily unpicked and doesn't require the nylon to be cut as in other knots.

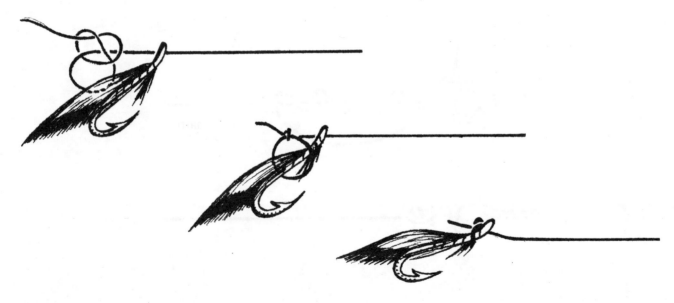

6. Flies

As we noted earlier, fly lines can seem very complex to the beginner. Flies can seem more bewildering still as there are literally thousands of different patterns. Anglers dream up new ones all the time. Some enjoy a fashionable notoriety for a season or two and are never heard of again. Others are unknown outside a certain country or locality. But others are widely known and have stood the test of time. In modern angling they all fall into one of four main categories: *streamers* or *lures*, which are tied to behave in the water like small fish; *wet flies*, traditionally the oldest form of fly but certainly still very useful; *floaters* or *dry flies* — these ones sit on the surface of the water; and *nymphs*, which represent the larvae of water-born insects.

A variety of hooks is used, ranging from the huge sizes used for saltwater gamefish through sizes 2-10 for streamers down to tiny 18s and 20s for some nymphs and dry flies. In practice this need not be confusing because a particular fly will only be available in a popular size range. When fishing, however, it is advisable to carry a fly in two or three sizes. If the fish are not taking it may not mean that you're using the wrong pattern — just the wrong size.

Streamer flies or lures

The forms which streamer flies may take are many and varied, but no matter what their construction, the majority suggest small bait fish and are fished to represent them. They are normally fished on sinking lines and are especially effective for catching large trout and can be very deadly, especially if used after dark. When retrieved through fast water they can be effective darting back and forth through the current as the angler retrieves his line in short jerks.

One of the more popular styles of streamer fly is the bucktail, made of deer hair. Other types of

A selection of favourite lures

The lure is the largest type of trout fly we use. This category includes the matuku and streamer types as well as the side-winged lures we know as killers. Other styles may be purely fancy with no pretensions to imitation of natural food at all.

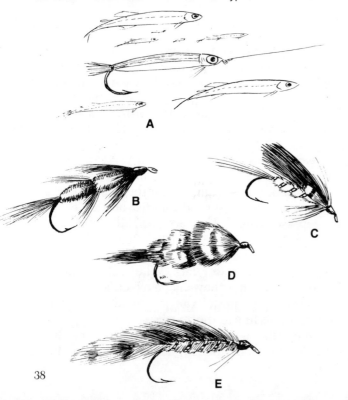

A However with some of the slim patterns there is a definite attempt to suggest small minnows. The Dollfly is one such and it is tied to suggest a smelt. The angler gives it movement and dash in retrieving it, and this proves the undoing of the trout.

B The Red Setter, an orange-bodied fly with brown hackles and tail. Rainbows love it. It's a good day fly, and I've also found it to be successful after dark.

C The Scotch Poacher, with its orange body and hackle, black tail and dark blue wings of pukeko feather (or substitute), is a favourite night fly. So are its cousins, the Taihape Tickler and Craig's Night-time.

D The Mrs Simpson, tied from cock pheasant rump feathers. This fly is tied in the killer style. The Hamill's Killer and the Lord's Killer are tied in the same way, with Hamill's using partridge or mallard dyed green while Lord's uses the barred plumage of the woodcock.

E Matuku flies are so called because the feathers of the matuku or New Zealand bittern were once used. Nowadays cock hackle feathers are used instead, tied along the shank with tinsel ribbing to prevent them from wrapping around the hook during casting. The feathers wriggle enticingly. Many variations of feather colour and body colour are possible.

natural hair may be used as well as several good synthetic materials. Some species of small fish are gold or silvery, others blue and silver — others dappled, some quite dark in appearance, so there is a demand for hair of differing colour either natural or dyed.

Feather streamers fall into several types. The New Zealand matuku style of fly has become very popular on the world fly fishing scene. This fly, with the feather wing held down by tinsel ribbing, is especially suited to fly casting as there is less tendency for the feather to wrap around the bend of the hook.

The eastern streamer so favoured by the New England fly fishermen of the U.S.A., is an excellent pattern for trolling but less favoured by fly casters, as the free wing tends to wrap around the hook. To overcome this, many tiers use a long shank hook. They also believe this causes less nipping of the fly by fish as "short takers" are caught by the hook protruding from the back of the fly.

The marabou streamer is another favourite pattern, the soft plumes being extremely receptive to any nuance of the river current which causes them to flutter in the water. When used in still water they open and close as the angler retrieves them.

Wet flies
The traditional wet flies have a very ancient lineage and some of the popular patterns in use today have pedigrees hundreds of years old. They are tied to represent water flies and land flies and were often cast with several being used at the same time. They were attached to droppers from the main leader and were referred to as a "team". Wet flies may be fished upstream and allowed to drift back but more commonly they are cast across or down and are taken by the fish as the line swings around in the current.

Besides certain dressings which obviously copy natural insects, many wet-fly patterns are fancy, representing nothing in particular. Some are quite fancy — especially if we take into account such patterns as the Teal and Silver, Peter Ross, Parmachene Belle and Montreal. It was from bright patterns like these that the salmon and sea trout flies evolved.

Except in special circumstances, they are fished

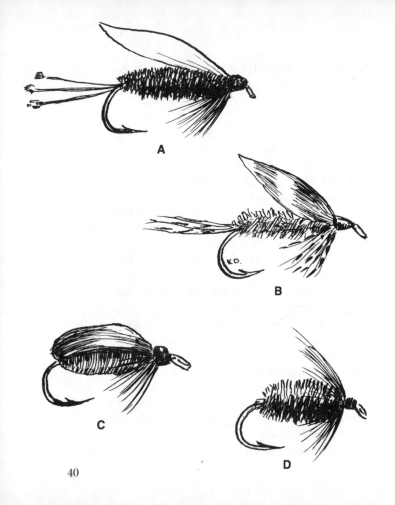

A

B

C

D

Wet flies

Wet flies are most popular in sizes 10, 12 and 14. These small flies used to be fished three or four to a leader but modern practice is to use only one, occasionally two. The four patterns shown here are useful everywhere.

A The Coachman. It is the poorer cousin of its flashy kinsman the Royal Coachman which is the same in all respects except that it has a bright red floss section in the middle of its body.

B The March Brown. With a body of hare's fur, a wing of hen pheasant and a hackle of brown partridge, it has remained unchanged for centuries. It is probably one of the most underrated flies we have and it is just as deadly today as it was in the time of Walton — and even long before that.

C The Beetle. Simple to tie, the dressing is changed to suit the particular species being copied. The brown beetle and green beetle are well represented with this dressing.

D Wales's gift to the angling world. The Coch-y-Bondhu is an all-round pattern that can be varied to suit the occasion. Tied plump it goes well when beetles abound and I know some anglers who tie it slim and use it during the evening rise when the mayfly are on the water.

Wet flies don't enjoy the favour they once did. They have been supplanted to a large extent by nymphs but every once in a while an angler re-discovers their true worth.

on sinking lines. They are fished on floating lines only under conditions of extreme low water or along lake margins where there is shallow water or beds of weeds where the fly must not be allowed to fish too deep for fear of snagging.

Many fly fishermen catch their first trout on a wet fly and I was no exception. My first trout came to a Leadwing Coachman which I was drifting down the current. Before my casting reached reasonable proficiency I would wade out into the river and peel off line into the current, allowing the flow to swim my fly for me. My favourite fly patterns were Hardy's Favourite, March Brown and Red-tipped Governor.

Dry flies or floaters

"Floater" is a good name for a dry fly as it more aptly describes the manner in which the fly is fished. Last century anglers discovered that a wet fly freshly tied on would sometimes float for two or three casts before it became wet and sank under the surface. They also knew that if a trout was feeding on insects floating on the surface of the stream, the best chance of catching it was to tie on a fresh fly which of course was dry, and then present it to the fish.

In time anglers discovered how to tie a fly with stiff hackles which supported it upon the surface tension of the water. The fly was oiled to prevent it becoming waterlogged and the fly line and gut greased to prevent a sinking line from pulling the fly under. Many of the popular dry flies used today were designed nearly 100 years ago and we have found no need to alter their dressings. However in the last 30 or 40 years we have seen some new and very successful floaters become universal favourites.

The majority of the old style of flies were designed to imitate water-born insects such as those of the *mayfly* group (Ephemeroptera) and the *caddis* (Trichoptera). The duns and spinner patterns covered the first group while sedges covered the *caddis* family (*sedge* is the term used by many anglers to denote the adult caddis).

However, there are several other water-born groups which are of more importance in some countries than they were on the chalk streams of southern England where the dry fly developed.

So in the mid-west of North America we have the *stonefly* playing a very important part on the

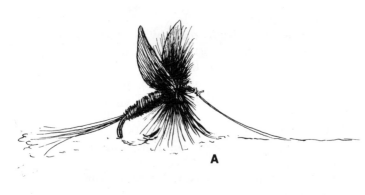

A

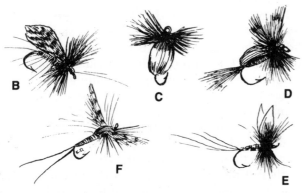

B

C

D

F

E

Dry flies

Some regard dry-fly fishing as the most enjoyable of all the forms of fly fishing. There can be no doubt that to watch a trout cruise up to the surface and gulp in your floating fly is a great thrill. Artificial dries are tied to cover a wide range of insects.

A The Twilight Beauty, a popular fly with its black body, brown hackles and grey wings. The hackles of dry flies need to be stiff to support the fly in the surface film. The flies are dunked in a special oil dressing to make them water-repellent and are false-casted vigorously between presentations to dry off any water adhering to the fly.

B A Sedge or Caddis fly, imitating one of the little moth-like insects you'll see skittering across the surface of the pool in the evening.

C A Beetle, plump and with a good hackle to help keep it floating on the surface.

D A deer-hair fly called the Humpie. It's probably the best all-round dry fly I have ever known. Being made of deer hair, which is hollow, it floats well.

E A favourite pattern the world over representing one of the mayfly species. It is the Greenwell's Glory.

F A sad little fly. It's one of my own dressings of the spent spinner. The female mayfly, after her dance above the mating pool, lays her eggs. Then, weak and dying, she drifts down the current spreadeagled upon the surface.

fly fisher's stage. In that part of the world the stonefly grows to great size and is very prolific so that it is of major importance to the trout, both in the nymphal and certainly in its winged form. In Australia and New Zealand caddis have a very major place in the diet of the trout.

But water-born insects are not the be all and end all of a trout's diet. As scientists point out to us, the world is very much the domain of the insects and we have a countless horde of land-born insects which anglers call *terrestrials*. These include every type of insect, winged or not, which might conceivably end up upon the surface of a stream or lake.

Obviously certain insects predominate at certain times of the year, and according to the district, anglers the world over have designed floaters to imitate these insects. These may be bees, wasps, ants, beetles, blowflies, cicadas, grasshoppers, leap hoppers, locusts, spiders — you name it.

Most of the flies used to imitate many of these species are quite large and to obtain bulk, peacock herl has long been a favourite. But by far the best floaters are those employing the use of deer hair.

Hollow, light and easy to use once certain difficulties have been overcome, deer hair can be used in a variety of shades either natural or dyed. It is used bunched or spun on and clipped to shape.

With this type of fly a stiff floating hackle is nowhere near as important and I have used successfully floaters I made of just spun deer hair, clipped to the shape of a cicada body. The result floated well with no dressing required and the trout really take it well when cicadas are dropping onto the water during bright summer days.

Using floaters is fun and to many anglers, just watching a trout come up through the water to take their fly is reward enough. After that initial thrill, all that follows is anti-climax.

Nymphs
In angling parlance the term nymph is used to describe the larva of any insect which lives in water. In many respects and especially in regard to the caddis group, this term is incorrect but owing to common usage and as a form of simplification, "nymph" is now regarded generally as being an acceptable description.

Nymphs

"Nymph" is the general term given to the larvae of all insects which spend their time under water prior to hatching. When mature they swim or crawl to the surface, the nymph splits open and a winged insect emerges. Nymphs form an important part of a trout's diet. They are to be found in all clean waters, running and still.

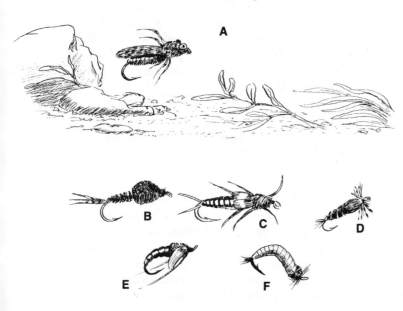

A The mudeye, a style of nymph tied to represent the larvae of the members of the dragonfly group. They are common in all still waters, being more abundant if there is a good bottom cover of weeds. They also live in slower-moving streams and I once discovered a very large specimen in a fast mountain stream. It is a very killing pattern in summer fished slowly on a floating line or, if fishing a drop-off, a slow sinking line will help to get it down to where the fish are cruising. I have also had considerable success on this pattern at night.

B The ever-popular Sawyer's Pheasant tail. With its heavy thorax of copper wire the Pheasant tail is a great pattern to fish through pockety fast water. It also sinks well in the deep slower holes.

C A Stonefly nymph. Tied using "Swannundaze", a plastic quill imitation, this lifelike nymph is very popular.

D An Olive nymph. Tied using olive-dyed seal's fur and partridge hackle, this pattern is useful in suggesting some of the mayfly-type nymphs.

E A Sedge or Caddis nymph. Fished in the evening on a floating line and given an occasional short twitch, to suggest the struggling natural, this pattern is deadly when the trout are feeding on hatching caddis flies.

F A Caddis grub made of latex rubber wound over a body of lead wire. This pattern is fished upstream and allowed to tumble back among the stones. It's a very useful pattern when the trout are feeding on the bottom of the stream, which is most of the time.

As a result we tend to lump together nymphs proper, larvae and pupae under the one heading.

Some of the more common forms of nymph to be found in running water are:

Common name	Scientific name
Mayflies (whether they hatch in May or not)	Emphemeroptera
Caddis flies	Trichoptera
Stoneflies	Plecoptera
Alders	Neuroptera
Craneflies	Diptera

In still water we find the following common groups:

Dragonflies	Odonata
Damselflies	Odonata
Midges	Diptera
Stillwater caddis	Trichoptera
Water beetles	Coleoptera
Hover flies	Diptera
Pond moths	Lepidoptera
Mosquitoes	Diptera
Craneflies	Diptera

All of these groups are common the whole world over, some of them assuming differing importance from country to country. Their

A weighted nymph
Tied on the author's patented double-shanked hook, this style of nymph is deadly. Tied with a mixture of pheasant tail, turkey and peacock herl and ribbed with copper wire, it drifts deeply through the lies among fast and broken water.

predominance may be affected by altitude or even specialised characteristics of certain waters in the same locality.

Much of this is determined by the quality of the water and the nature of the bottom. A river with a sand and gravel bed will prove a suitable habitat for certain insects which may not be so readily found in a fast bouldery stream. Water temperature also plays a very important part in determining just exactly what type of insect finds a habitat to its preference.

The same applies to lakes. A high-country lake set among snow mountains will have a different balance of fauna than will a lowland lake with marshy margins and rich weed beds.

So the nymph angler has a whole spectrum of insects and their behaviour to imitate. Don't be put off by the Latin names and the scientific theory. It's not difficult to get to know the insect life of your favourite stretch of water and choose your nymphs accordingly.

Fly tying

Trout flies have long been the subject of mysticism and the materials used in some of the old fly patterns were kept secret by their makers. Not so today — there are countless books on the subject which all give the dressings used in many fly patterns. Modern fly fishers tie their own flies and a range of materials gathered from all corners of the world is available for their use. I must make a personal appeal to all anglers never to use any plumage or fur from a threatened species.

Fur and feather from domestic or legitimate game species are readily available as well as some interesting synthetics and they will kill as well as if not better than some of the so-called wonder plumages.

Tying flies is not as difficult as some would believe, and the art can be mastered with a little care and patience. One of the great angling thrills which can only be experienced once is to catch that first trout on a fly of your own making.

There are several good manuals available from your nearest bookstore or tackle dealer and if a supply of tools or materials is not readily available in your own home town there are mail-order houses the world over which specialise in supplying the wide range of gear.

The great thing about fly tying is that it allows you to indulge your own personal fancies and theories, and often these new and weird creations can prove to be real fish killers. The expenditure on a kit of fly-tying gear need not be large, as the necessary tools can be purchased and materials added to the kit as your skill progresses.

7. Casting and retrieving

The overhead cast
Remember — you'll never make a good delivery if your back cast isn't right.

So we're going to begin by making good back casts. Once you've got that right the rest follows on. Get yourself out on the lawn. I'm assuming that you'll be using a single-handed rod and that you're right-handed.

The grip
A rod should feel comfortable when held in the hand. Unfortunately when you are just setting out you're not really sure what is and what isn't right. You are too easily persuaded by others, since as a beginner you feel everyone knows more than you do. But one thing you can do is tell if the rod is balanced. It should lie nicely in the hand and not be tip-heavy or butt-heavy. There are many old reels still in service which were made to balance old split cane rods but some of these beautiful old reels have too much metal in them for modern rods. Modern reels balance modern rods.

Grasp the grip with the thumb along the top. The thumb serves several purposes. It enables you to take a positive grip of the rod and this is vital for control. It enables you to use it as a backstop to bring your rod to a halt at the correct moment. And it enables you to apply the delivery drive as you complete the forward cast.

Some anglers as they make the back cast tend to

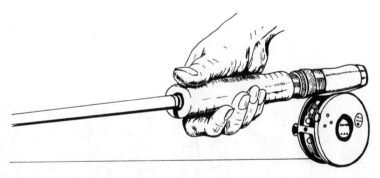

The overhead cast

The composite illustration shows a complete overhead cast. It is the basis of all other casts and has to be thoroughly learnt.

A starts with the rod tip held low. **B** and **C** have the rod tip rising. **D** has begun to lift the line and then **E,** the heavily outlined figure, flicks the rod back with a sharp movement of the wrist. The rod is locked at that position and at **F** and **G** the line, drawn by the sudden impetus, is thrown up high over the angler's shoulder in a back-rolling loop. At **H** the line has straightened out behind the angler and at that precise instant he begins the forward cast. Now **I,** the

second heavily outlined figure, puts on the power. This is done by pushing down with the thumb and wrist and bringing the rod to a horizontal position as smartly as possible (**J**).

At **K** the line should then fall onto the surface in a relatively straight line. Delicacy is achieved by releasing the line with the left hand just as it straightens over. If this isn't done the line is liable to spring back towards the angler and drop to the surface in a big snaky S. When beginning, the left hand serves to anchor the 10 m or so of line which you are casting. Keep it at your side, don't allow it to follow the reel back and forth as though it was tied to the rod butt. *Keep that left hand down. Wait until the line has straightened out behind you before you start the forward cast. Try and accomplish the cast in a steady unjerky manner.*

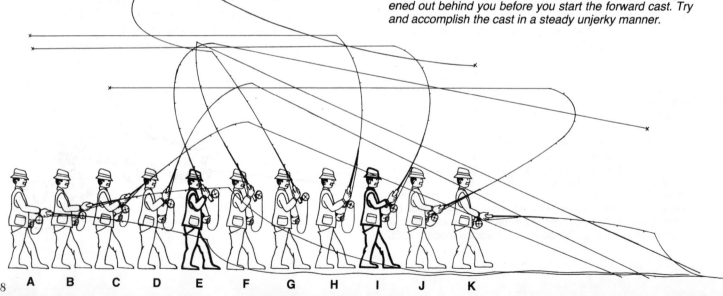

48   **A**   **B**   **C**   **D**   **E**   **F**   **G**   **H**   **I**   **J**   **K**

roll the thumb (and the rod) slightly inwards. Others tend to hold the thumb slightly to the left on the inside top of the grip, then roll the rod slightly as it comes back so that their thumb is in the backstop position.

To practise casting, strip off about 10 m of line, which is ample to start. To the end of your leader you will have attached an old fly from which the bend has been removed with a pair of side-cutters, or take a piece of pale knitting yarn and tie a tuft to the end of the nylon.

Make sure the line is lying straight on the ground in front of you. Start at the slightly aggressive stance with the left foot forward (left-handers reverse pose) and make sure your rod tip is held low, just above the ground. This is important as you are going to need the rod tip to begin work by pulling on the line from the moment you lift it. Anchor the line with the left hand and keep this by your side. Now look at the illustration. Rod tip down, line straight out in front.

Now we're ready to begin the cast. Start by lifting the rod back to the side of your shoulder in a nice smooth motion and when at 10 o'clock snap the wrist back so that the rod carries on to the vertical position. In practice you'll find it carries on back to about 1 o'clock due to the flex in the rod. You only use your forearm and then your wrist. Don't worry about photographs you've seen of fly casters with their arms extended to full length, with great loops of line sailing through the air. Those guys are long-distance casting. We're only trying to cast 10 m and you've not made a very good job of that yet.

Let's do it again. Run your line straight out in front, rod tip low. Start lifting with the forearm then snap with the wrist. Stop the rod — don't go back too far — and there: the line flows out behind over your shoulder and rolls out in a smooth flowing loop.

Let the line drop to the ground behind you, turn around and then do it in the opposite direction. Once you can do that you can make the forward cast. You only have to wait until the line has straightened out behind you before you begin, so watch over your shoulder — you'll see that it takes a couple of seconds for the line to straighten out. If you make your forward cast too soon the line will crack like a whip. If you hear that line crack when you're casting it means either that you've pulled your fly off on a branch behind you or you've begun your forward cast too soon — in which case you may still have lost your fly by cracking it off.

So let's try that again. Start with rod tip low, smooth motion back with the forearm and then that snap back of the wrist. Wait for the line to straighten out behind . . . then bring the rod forward with the forearm and drive the tip down with the wrist and pushing with the thumb. Stop the rod in the horizontal position and the line should roll over and land in a straight line in front of you.

Sounds easy, doesn't it? Well, from experience I know some people find it easier to learn than others. Some seem born with the knack, others only acquire it with great difficulty. It is all timing and the correct application of force. It is not a jerky action but a smooth rhythm that brings the rod into play and utilises its spring. When we begin the back cast we are "loading" the rod. The tip resists the backward movement as the weight of the line comes upon it but then as it loads up the inherent spring of the rod, plus momentum, takes over and a carefully executed snap of the

wrist shoots it through the gravity barrier into a good high back cast. Once the line is straight out behind a smooth forward movement loads the rod once more, and the forward snap of the wrist enables the line to roll over nicely in front.

All this time the left hand has anchored the line against your side. Don't follow the reel backwards and forwards with the left hand. When you can cast about 15 m without any trouble we'll show you how that left hand can really come into play, so that with practice you'll be making casts of up to 30 m. But for the moment keep that left hand down at your side where it belongs.

Keep up your practice with the overhead cast. Remember the cardinal rule — a good straight back cast means a good forward cast to follow. Don't worry too much about accuracy at this stage; that will come in time.

Now let's look at some of the things which could be going wrong.

If the line comes up off the ground and hits you in the face or wraps around the rod, you are either doing things too slowly or you have too much line out. If the first is the case, speed up that pick-up into a smooth lift, running into the snap back of the wrist. If the second is the case, then shorten your line. You may be one of the characters I often meet who seem to pull a few more centimetres unconsciously from the reel every time they make a cast. This is because they grasp the line too close to the reel, with the result that every time they lift the rod more line is pulled off.

Perhaps you're hitting the rod with your line during the forward cast. There are several reasons why this may happen.

It may be that you're not letting the line straighten out on the back cast before bringing the rod forward, thus jerking the uncompleted loop down on to the rod. More likely is that you've dropped your rod back too far when making the back cast so that as well as hitting the ground behind you, the line comes through on a low trajectory and as well as striking the rod it may well wrap itself around your head and neck. (Now you know why we suggested snipping your fly off at the bend before we started practising.)

Another cause of the line striking the rod is one seldom found in raw beginners but likely to make itself apparent as a degree of competence is reached. This is also something which is liable to happen when our angler begins dry-fly fishing, which involves aerial false casting to dry the fly. The cause of the problem is simply stopping the rod too soon on the forward cast. Gravity is beginning to drop the back cast and it will catch on the rod if it hasn't been carried far enough forward during the delivery stroke.

This problem of the line striking the rod can be overcome to a fair extent by holding the rod out at an angle from the shoulder. However, there could very well be another reason for sloppy casting and disastrous results, and that is tired muscles. Once your wrist, arm or shoulder starts to bother you it's time to stop and either have a rest or pack it in for the day.

Fly casting is supposed to be fun, and once you've mastered certain basic rudiments you'll really enjoy making good casts and feeling the rod and fly line working as a unit. You can tell you're doing things right when that line tells you it really wants to go. So don't make a chore of it. None of us ever became proficient casters during our first lesson. It's something you'll acquire with dedicated practice — and remember: rest that arm when it needs it.

The side cast

The side cast is literally the overhead cast laid on its side. It is a very useful style of cast when the line has to be kept low to avoid overhanging branches. It is also the cast to use when you need to place your fly under overhanging bushes, as well as being a way to avoid strong winds.

I always find that if I have to punch a cast into a breeze, I can do so much better with a side cast. I have also found it to be a very accurate way to cast, and if the line is stopped with a slight jerk the line curls around to the left. This can be an ideal way to present a fly to a fish without showing it too much line.

The side cast

You're going to find plenty of occasions when this cast will help you. There's nothing tricky to it. Once a reasonable standard of casting has been achieved it's a natural progression. It's also a handy way to keep the fly's passage away from the body on windy days.

The backhand cast

Sooner or later you're going to find yourself in the situation where you are fishing on the wrong side of the river and high banks or trees make the use of a backhand cast imperative.

This is an awkward cast to make and there are times when I wish I was ambidextrous. However, as with all forms of casting, practice is the answer and some people become very adept at it. When possible though, I use the reverse cast.

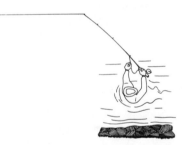

The backhand cast

Instead of being able to cast across our regular shoulder we sometimes have to throw the back cast across the other shoulder. I have always found this to be awkward but there are times when there is no choice. The timing is the same as for a regular overhead cast. Practise it so that when you have to use it you won't botch up a critical cast. I dislike having to use the backhand to cast an accurate fly to an easily frightened fish rising in a clear, low, bright stream.

The reverse cast

I don't know why I didn't think of this one years ago, it's so simple. All you do is modify your stance.

Suppose you're fishing your way upstream. Well, instead of facing squarely on to your target area, adopt a side-on stance and crab your way up the stretch of water. In this way you reverse your casting procedure and your back cast becomes your forward cast and vice versa, with the delivery being made on the back cast. With a little practice this method can be very accurate and, more important, it is an ideal cast to make where your back cast has to be directed through trees or other obstructions. It also permits you to tighten on a fish much better than when you have your forearm across your body. Crabbing along a stream edge using this cast a lot of water can be fished in ease, whereas a frontal attack can be downright awkward.

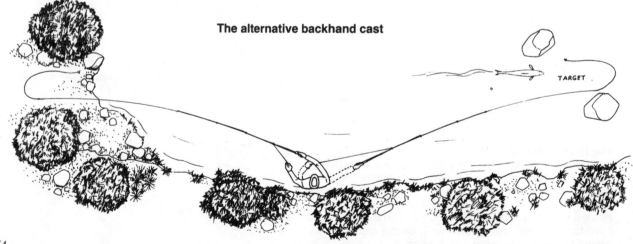

The alternative backhand cast

TARGET

The high back cast or steeple cast

This simply involves throwing your back cast very high to overcome shrubs or other obstructions. To achieve this, angle your arc of power downwards so that there is a tendency for the line to hit the water less delicately than is the case with a regular cast. Most anglers prefer to use a roll cast in these situations. However, it should be practised as there will be occasions when roll-casting will not be practical, such as when fishing a sinking fly line. It isn't possible to cast very far using this style, but it is useful in restricted circumstances.

The steeple cast

The roll cast

All fly anglers need to know how to roll-cast, as it is a very important facet of line control. It is a very easy cast to perfect and when some of my pupils have problems with regular casting I find many of them are able to progress through the medium of the roll cast. If we were to roll-cast all the time we would use more flexible rods than are generally used. The old style of split-cane wet-fly rod was ideally suited to this.

It is an essential cast for picking line off the water and when I have pupils perfecting their upstream techniques, it is the first step in aerialising line.

Most make the mistake of bringing their rods back too quickly when beginning the roll. The rod is raised slowly from the horizontal position, so as not to lift the line from the water, and stopped at 2 o'clock.

Then there is a pause for a second as the angler waits for the weight of the line to drop behind the rod. Then when this has happened the rod is driven over and out to the horizontal position again. The line will roll over nicely and lie out straight as can be, carrying the fly and dropping on to the water with a minimum of splash. About 10 m of line is an ideal length, although with the correct rig and a following wind, long distances can be cast.

Floating lines can be roll-cast off the water better than sinking ones, as the latter have to be drawn up through the water first and the "grip" of the water must be broken — sometimes two roll casts in succession must be made to get a sinking line free of water tension. Otherwise shorten your line if you want to avoid the risk of breaking your rod.

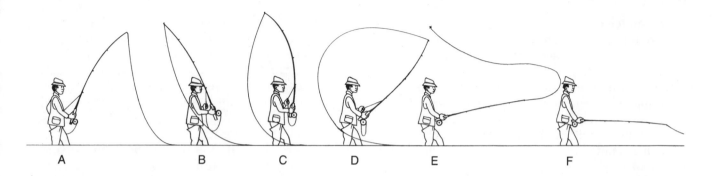

A   B   C   D   E   F

The roll cast

This cast has to be learnt as it becomes an integral part of all-round casting. With practice and a good following wind an angler can make roll casts of 20 m or more.

You begin with about 10 m or so of line out, then raising the rod tip slowly you bring the rod back from A to B. Then you must wait a second or two until the line has dropped down below the tip. See how the line is drooping down behind the angler's shoulder at B?

Now C, D, E and F are all one smooth movement. The rod is pushed up and over with the thumb providing the power of the cast. The line should roll over easily and lay straight on the water in front of you.

We use the roll cast in two ways. The first is to get your fly across the water to where the trout are. Extra line can be released by the left hand and this will shoot through the guides increasing the length of the cast. This cast is essential in water where a high background or trees make a regular overhead cast impossible.

The second use of a roll cast is at the end of a drift or retrieve when the line is rolled, not onto the water but into the air when it becomes the prelude to a regular overhead cast.

The snatch cast

Here is a cast which has often enabled me to shoot low up under overhanging trees in a manner impossible with any of the regular casts. I also use it on occasions to show a student with casting trouble how to get a fly upstream on a long drift without too much difficulty. To fish this way continually is rather slow but if your standard of casting is not very good it will give you the chance to hook a fish — and believe me, many do who wouldn't otherwise.

The method is very simple and ideally suited for upstream nymphing in faster waters. Merely allow 12 m or so of floating line to trail downstream and with your arm extended back, drop your rod tip right down to the surface of the water. Then lift the rod with increasing speed and snatch your line from the water. The tension of the water on the line draws the rod tip down to start and then when the spring of the rod overcomes the resistance of the water the line shoots forward and over. With a little practice you can cast quite accurately this way. If you wish to cast across the stream a little you merely complete the forward throw by aiming the tip of your rod in the direction you want your fly to land. After each drift is completed it is necessary to allow the retrieved line to be drawn out again by the current passing below you. This takes a while to happen, and you only get about one cast to every three completed in the normal manner. But it does have a bonus: every now and then you will hook a fish on the drift below you, so always be ready for it.

A word of warning — this method of upstream fishing can be disastrous for your rod with a sinking line if you try to lift too much. A floating line may be snatched off the surface with relative ease but the same length of sinking line completely immersed in the water is another matter, so beware — unless you want to risk breaking your rod.

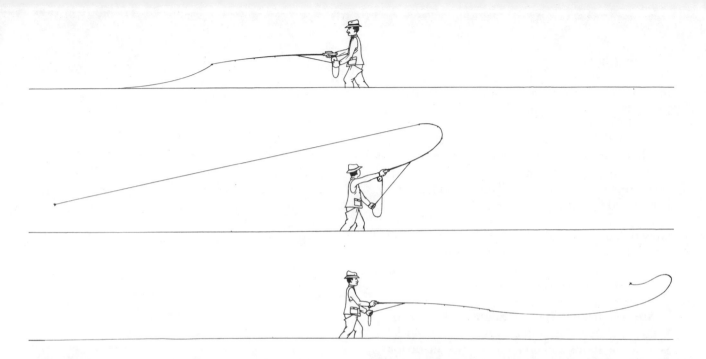

The snatch cast

The principle of this cast is an easy one. The line is allowed to drift downstream until it is floating in a straight line directly below you. Lower your rod tip to the water, then with a pull of the left hand (to speed up the lift of the line) and an upstream throw with the rod you can throw the line upstream to land in the direction the angle of the rod has dictated to it. This cast only has application when fishing upstream. It is useful when upstream nymphing with a floating line. Some streams flow under avenues of over-hanging trees and any other type of cast is almost impossible. It takes a bit of practice to achieve accuracy but it comes after a while. Of course it can be used in open water as well.

Proficient anglers consider it bad form, and some purists classify it as being reprehensible. But if it helps you to catch a trout, go to it. There'll be plenty of opportunities to indulge in fancy casting later on.

59

The slingshot cast

Here is a cast which really verges on the category of trick. Its use is extremely limited and only practical on small streams heavily overhung with trees. I have seldom had to use it but then again I don't fish the sort of water very often where it would be useful. I find that with a 2.4 m rod I can project my fly about 6 m with the slingshot cast. To do this I take hold of my fly line and leave the leader and fly dangling.

Now that covers all the basic methods of casting of which I am aware. The two to practise most are the roll cast and the overhead cast. Once you have mastered these the rest come easily.

Let's recap.

Are you making a good straight back cast? Are you using your wrist and making that rod work for you? Make it flex and do the job it was made for. Don't treat it as though it's a fragile little stick. Lay on just the right amount of power at the right time and casting will become easy and a real delight.

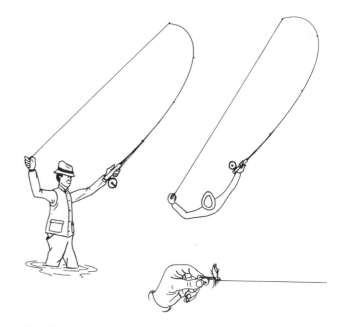

The slingshot cast

This cast has limited application as the distance which can be covered is limited to the length of your rod and your arms. It can be put to use when fishing small overgrown streams enabling a fly to be flicked into a small pocket where any other type of cast would be impossible. Be very careful how you grip the fly.

The angler is about to punch the line forward — but not before the backcast has fully straightened out behind him.

RETRIEVING

So you're casting 10 or 15 m with ease now?
Before we look at ways to increase your distance
you have to learn to retrieve line. This can be
done by several methods.

Coiling

The line is simply drawn in by the left hand in
loops, and you must take care to coil the line
regularly so that the loops don't cross and tangle
each other as they're released during the "shoot".
Use the thumb to hold the loops in position and
also to control their release.

When retrieving line, either by looping or the
methods we're about to describe, you'll find it
easier to draw the line across the index finger on
the right hand. Between draws the index finger
traps the line against the rod handle so that the
line is always under control should a fish take your
fly.

When you want to retrieve line quickly,
especially when fishing upstream in fast water,
you draw it in large loops. But if you are fishing a
deep sunken nymph or streamer downstream or
over a weed bed in a lake you may want to make a
slow jerky retrieve and this may be done in
several ways. Perhaps the most successful is
knitting.

Coiling line

To retrieve a fly fished downstream, or
to take in slack line when casting a
nymph or dry fly upstream, it is necessary to draw in the line in manageable
coils so that it can slip easily from the
fingers when being re-cast.

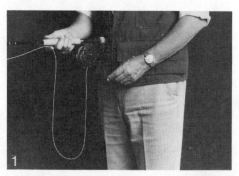

1 The line is placed over the index
finger of the casting hand.

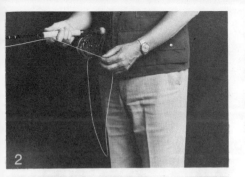

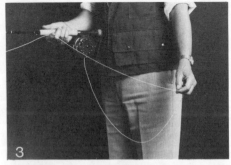

2 The line is taken between the thumb and index finger of the other hand. Note the amount of slack between the hand and the reel. It is important to allow for this slack which enables the rod to be lifted for a backcast without pulling more line from the reel.

3 The left hand draws half a metre or more of line over the index finger of the rod hand.

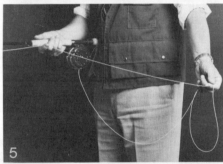

4 The left hand then moves back to take hold of the line again forming a loop.

5 The left hand draws another length of line through the guides.

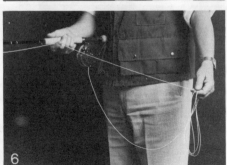

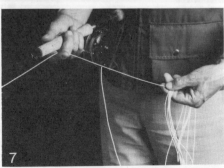

6 The process is repeated until several coils are held. Note how the thumb controls the placement of the line.

7 At this stage the angler is ready to cast again. Since the coils are neatly placed beside each other they will slip from under the thumb when pressure is released. The line is dropped off the index finger of the right hand before the cast is made.

Knitting

This method takes a little time to accomplish readily but once mastered it's never forgotten. Now look at the illustrations.

Firstly, always grasp the line so that there is a good loop hanging between your left hand and the reel. If you don't pay attention to this little detail you are going to find that when you begin the cast you lift your rod back and either your left hand pulls more line from the reel or, more likely, one of the under coils in your left hand is pulled out, laying the foundation for a snarled line when you want it to shoot. With experience it is possible to handle up to 20 m of line using this method.

When I was a youngster I used to carry a length of cord in my pocket with a loop on the end. Whenever I got the chance, I would hang it on a doorknob or on the back of a chair and start practising. It was well worth the effort. In no time at all I trained my fingers to do something which is now second nature to me.

This retrieve is an important one as you can fish your fly back at a slow crawl, with little jerks or at a good steady draw once you have learned to do it swiftly.

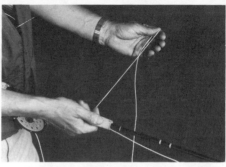

1 As with coiling, the line is best drawn across the index finger of the right hand. The line is taken across the index finger and held with the thumb and palm open. Make sure you have ample line between the reel and your left hand.

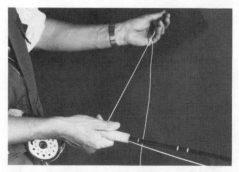

5 The lower fingers are opening as the hand prepares to move back again.

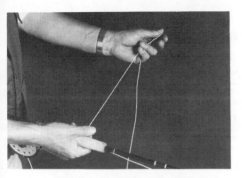

2 The third and little fingers then close over to hold the line in place.

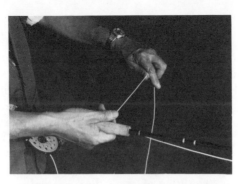

3 Then the hand rolls over and takes the line between the thumb and index finger again.

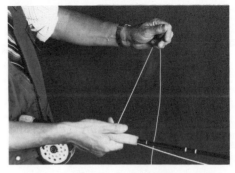

4 The hand rolls back again with the line held by the two lowest fingers.

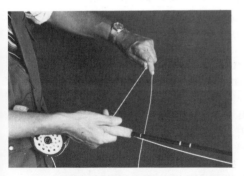

6 The thumb and index finger are taking hold on another loop.

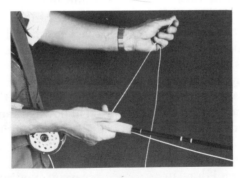

7 The hand has now moved back; you can see the even loops of line forming in the hand.

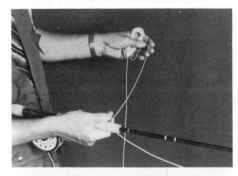

8 The hand is full of loops and ready to recast. The loops slip out from under the thumb which controls delivery through the pressure it applies.

The reef
This is another method I have seen used. It is very simple — the line is wound around the closed fingers just as you might roll up a ball of yarn when knitting.

The "combination" retrieve
When I am fishing a very long line, such as downstream drifting with a sinking line or casting over still water with a floater, I have 30 or 40 m of line to control and that means I have about 20 m to handle as retrieve. This is a lot to handle and then shoot successfully, so I find it easier to use a combination of retrieves.

First I make several draws and have one loop consisting of four draws. Then a loop of three draws. Then another of two draws. As each draw is about 1 m that means I have nearly 10 m under control for a start. If you make a big loop and then progressively smaller ones you will find that they shoot better with less inclination to tangle.

After these loops I begin to knit my retrieve and do this with another 6 m or so. Then I draw in another couple of loops and find that this handles

just right for shooting. I shoot these last loops on my first false cast, perhaps half the knitted retrieve on the second false cast, and then by hauling (a technique explained in the next section) and putting everything into it, I get the rest away with the delivery punch of my last cast. Every once in a while I get a snarl but I find this method keeps it to a minimum.

So practise your retrieving as it is essential for line control and delivery when making long casts.

MAKING LONG CASTS
Some anglers go through most of their lives making casts of seldom more than 10 or 15 m, and that's just fine if your fly fishing is limited to small rivers and streams. They usually get any distance they need by feeding line into the water to be taken up by the current, and while they may have only cast 10 m, their fly will end up fishing 20 or 30 m downstream from them.

But some of the great fly fishing waters of the world are large, and if you are going to fish any stillwater areas, whether a loch, a lake or a reservoir, you are going to improve your chances of success if you can cast a decent distance.

To do this you use a technique known as hauling, and you need to learn the single haul and the double haul.

The single haul

As you have become more proficient with your casting, I don't doubt that you have pulled more and more line from your reel until at last you have literally had your line land on your head as you were unable to cope with all you had out. You have reached your overloading point. It was probably about 20-25 m, the overloading point for most people of average height and physique.

So how do we achieve greater distance? We do it simply by increasing the speed of the line to overcome gravity, and we do this by opening up

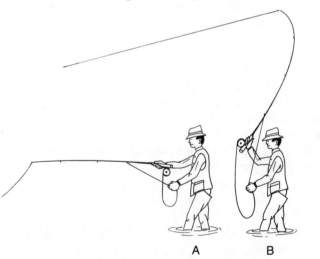

A   B   C

The single haul
A and B show the beginning of the back cast, and at C, the angler has pulled right down with the left hand while the right has frozen the rod in the back-cast position. When the line has straightened out behind him he makes his forward cast releasing the line from his left hand at the completion of the down drive. *Care must be taken not to release the line until the right hand has fully completed the down drive.* Beginners have a tendency to release the line from the left hand a fraction too soon. This ruins the cast and the line falls in a heap in front of the angler. With a bit of practice the haul becomes a natural part of every cast.

67

our chests — using the right arm as an extension of the rod to push the tip up higher, while at the same time drawing the line down swiftly with the left hand.

Whereas the line had been sulky and unwilling to remain airborne, it will now become responsive. This is the essence of the single haul. Try it and you'll be delighted — perhaps you have already discovered it for yourself. I know I had long before I read about it.

The double haul

Any angler who wants to make long casts has to master this technique. It has little application for the angler whose fishing is restricted to small streams but if you are fishing larger rivers and lakes then you'll need to practise it. Whenever I have had a pupil experiencing trouble with the double haul I've thought of the old trick we used to practise as youngsters of rubbing our chests and patting our heads at the same time. It wasn't easy to accomplish at first but sooner or later we got the hang of it. Double hauling is in the same category. You have to train your hands to do something that doesn't always come naturally.

But it's really quite simple and once mastered is never forgotten. The haul then becomes a part of every cast, as the use of the left hand to speed up the line helps in so many ways. For instance, when casting into a breeze, a smart pull with the left hand as the forward cast is being made will punch a fly into the wind when it would otherwise be blown back in its tracks.

Using a shooting head

A shooting head, or shooting taper, has already been described. The 10 m length is joined or spliced to about 30 m of fine "shooting" line which, because of its small diameter, creates less friction, air resistance and weight drag, enabling fly-casters to throw their lines a very long distance with relative ease. This shooting line may be monofilament or special plastic-coated floating backing.

You will find adherents of each kind of shooting line, and it largely depends on the style of fly fishing they engage in.

The problem with the shooting head is how to handle all that retrieved backing when the next cast is to be made. If you are casting from a boat,

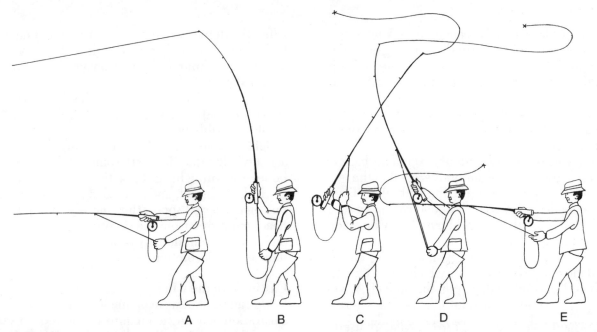

A   B   C   D   E

The double haul

A and B are the same as the single haul, but C shows the difference between the two casting techniques. As the line flows back the left hand, which is firmly gripping the line, rides up and allows the line to slip back through the rod guides. The left hand freezes at that position for a second or so, long enough for the line to straighten out fully behind. D

shows the next stage of the cast: the line is hauled down smartly by the left hand as the rod is brought forward for the forward cast. As the rod is brought down to the horizontal position, the left hand releases the line. The slack then shoots through the rod guides, pulled forward by the out-rolling motion of the line.

you can just lay a piece of canvas or sacking in the bottom of the boat and strip the running line on to it. If reasonable care is exercised the line pulls up from the bottom of the boat during the cast in the same sequence it was allowed to settle.

The same principle applies if you are fishing from a nice clean grassy bank or perhaps a large rocky outcrop.

But if you are standing among rough herbage or long rank grass such techniques are out of the question. So you can use a stripping basket. This may be made of canvas with a solid rim and a strap to attach it around your middle or it may be made of plastic, rather like a sort of clothes basket. Inventive types make their own, using any kind of mundane domestic container which will attach to a belt and sit comfortably upon the midriff. As you retrieve, the line is coiled into the basket where it lies neatly until the next cast is to be made.

Of course, many fly anglers wade to fish and in these circumstances the stripping basket is admirable — if you like them, which some anglers don't. They prefer to use the floating running line and let it hang in large loops upon the surface of the water. Since it floats it lifts off fairly easily when the delivery cast is made. Even so it takes a little experience to handle it well, but once you develop a technique you'll find you can cast very long distances indeed.

My personal opinion is that unless you are concerned with making extra-long casts, you would probably be better off with a weight-forward line. However, I must acknowledge that there are some fly casters who believe shooting heads to be the greatest thing since sliced bread, and instead of carrying spare line on extra reel spools they merely coil up the head, cut it free from the shooting line, produce one of a different density from their vest and knot it on as a replacement.

Casting into the wind
Wind can be the cause of much hard work and frustration. Casting a line into a wind requires the use of the haul, usually only employed in distance casting. But when a wind blowing downstream makes it difficult for an angler to place a fly only 10 or 15 m away, action must be taken.

First is to narrow the arc of the line loop. This is achieved by moving the rod through a very small arc from say 11 o'clock to 1 o'clock while at the same time giving the line impetus by pulling on it with the left hand on the forward stroke. This speeds up the delivery of the line and to a certain extent will help to overcome wind — although gale winds and sudden strong gusts make fishing difficult if not impossible. But in moderate winds this method will contribute a great deal towards making your casting more acceptable.

8. Fishing tactics

You're now equipped with the basic tackle. You know how to put it together and how to use it. But there is still an important element we have not yet discussed: the water itself.

By learning to "read" the water and developing some knowledge of trout habits you won't be so reliant on sheer chance. You will be able to look at a river or lake, make your own assessment of its "fishability" and select the appropriate tactics.

Wet or dry? Lure or nymph? Upstream or downstream? With experience and common sense the choices come more easily. But for the moment let's assume you arrive at the bank of a river or lake and don't know where to begin. On the following pages I have detailed some of the most typical kinds of fishing water, together with the usual tactics employed to persuade a fish to take your fly.

Where trout lie
Opposite is a bird's eye view of a section typical of streams everywhere. Note the boulder in the run leading into the pool. We all know that there is usually a good lie behind the boulder, but did you know that there's often a better one just above it? The force of the water hitting the obstruction causes a back pressure and the trout like to occupy this spot as they can maintain position with a minimum of effort.

The third trout down is lying at the edge of a small bar or drop off caused by the backswirl in the near edge. Always approach this part of the pool carefully and have several casts through the water before even attempting to wade in. Nine times out of ten, an angler will approach the head of a pool such as this, and wade out up to his knees frightening off what may well have been the best chance of the day. The other fish lie over the far side of the pool in the deeper water under the

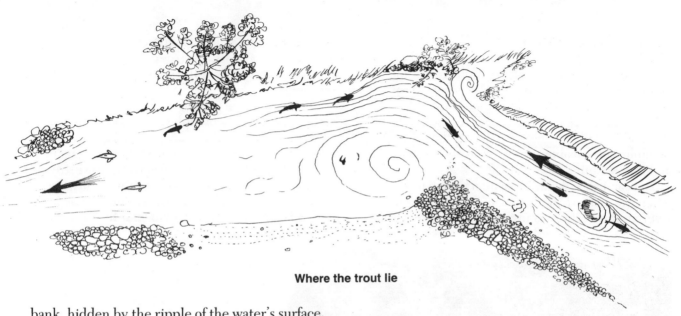

Where the trout lie

bank, hidden by the ripple of the water's surface. Note the fish lying under the overhanging branch. They love such spots. The tree or branch gives them a sense of security and well it may — getting a fly into such spots can be a very tricky business.

There are two fish shown in the glide at the bottom of the pool. You will sometimes find trout there during the day, especially if the river holds brown trout, but the reason I have included these is because it's a favourite feeding position for trout in the late evening and after dark. So if you're crossing the tail end of a pool in bad light or darkness, always fish the spot well before crossing. You might be in for a surprise.

Downstream lure fishing

This is probably the easiest style of fishing there is. The fishermen in the photograph are wading 20 m or so above a known lie in the river. They stand there for hours working their flies back and forth. If the trout are present and co-operative, the anglers will be successful. If not, then they'll be philosophical about it and enjoy the fresh air and the sunshine.

You can fish in a similar fashion if you know where the fish are likely to be. If not you can fish a river methodically, casting across the current and letting your line swing downstream. After every few casts, move a little further downstream. In this way you can cover the water pretty thoroughly.

This is the usual procedure for fishing wet flies, and can be used for nymph fishing too. When fishing a nymph in this manner on a floating line, however, you have to rely on sight more than feel. Follow the end of your line as it drifts downstream and if it seems to pause or move unnaturally then raise your rod to tighten the line. You cannot depend on *feeling* the fish take your fly.

Downstream lure fishing

Drifting a nymph
Small streams require a careful approach. The angler is drifting his nymph through a deeper pocket across the stream. Any hesitation in the line's natural drift will require an instant response from the angler — lifting the rod tip to tighten the line and set the hook.

Upstream nymphing

Another productive style of nymphing involves casting upstream and letting your nymph drift back towards you. As it does so you must strip the slack line in with your left hand so that you can be in immediate contact if a fish takes. The take will be signalled by a stopping or sideways pull of the end of the line. A pale-coloured line is an asset here as it is easier to see. In fact most floating lines are manufactured in pale colours. Some anglers use a bright-coloured indicator at the join between line and leader so that they can maintain watch on their line even in turbulent water.

Trout are lazy creatures. They prefer to select a nice spot behind a boulder or other irregularity in the stream bed and rest out of the current. The surface of the water may be flowing at a rate of knots but down below the water is full of negative and even reverse flows. It makes sense. The trout selects a place where it can maintain its position with a minimum of effort and just moves out to one side or the other to pick up any morsel the current washes past its post. So to catch these fish you must fish your fly near the bottom. That's why the weighted nymph is so popular. It gets down to where the trout are feeding.

There is only one reason why a trout will come up from its lazy little lie on the bottom of the river and that's a lot of free food coming down the stream. This happens every time there's a hatch of insects — caddis, mayflies, stoneflies, or whatever. It occurs on some streams during the day and on most during the evening. Then you can catch the trout on an unweighted nymph just under the surface. You use your floating line and grease most of your leader except the last 30 cm or so. Cast above the trout and watch your line and leader like a hawk. At the least suggestion of a take lift your rod and tighten. If you don't, the trout will eject the fly unless you are lucky enough to have the current pull it into the corner of the fish's mouth, when it will roll and twist in an effort to dislodge it.

Dry-fly fishing

Dry-fly fishing involves floating an artifical fly on the surface of the water in such a way that a trout will be fooled into taking it for a real insect. The flies are dressed with bushy stiff hackles which assist them to sit on the surface of the water. They

Upstream nymph fishing

In this photograph Gary Kemsley, a Taupo fishing guide, is fishing the "Boulder reach", a well-known stretch of the Tongariro River. When a fresh run is in the river fish can be found all up this stretch. The stony bottom is full of pockets which the trout favour as lies.

Fishing the weighted nymph

A nymphing trout

are dunked in a bottle of water-resistant dressing to prevent the fly from becoming waterlogged and are dried between casts with a vigorous swishing of the rod.

The method is best employed when trout are obviously rising to insects floating on the surface. They may be mayflies, caddis, beetles, grasshoppers or whatever insect is prevalent at the time, possibly a combination of two or more types. The best rise is usually in the evening but if enough insects are on the water trout will rise readily during the day.

The insects may be hatching from the water, drifting along the surface laying eggs or, on windy summer days, they may be blown on to the water from the surrounding countryside.

Trout don't feed in any old place in the river. They take up station where the flow of the river channels the drifting food into a narrow lane. You will recognise the small trout by their quick splashy rises; the bigger trout are more sedate and some of the quieter rises you see may well be from trout of trophy proportions.

Of course, a floating line is a necessity as is a finely tapered leader. You must be able to drop your fly with a fair measure of accuracy and absence of splash. Trout have a blind spot behind them and we use this to carefully move into position 10 m or so below the fish. As the light begins to fade you will be able to move in even closer than this.

The object is to cast your fly to land above the fish so that it will drift back over its lie. You must be careful not to drop your line over the fish, and the best situation is where you can cast up and across the stream at an angle of about 45 degrees. Drop your fly so that it drifts down on your side of the trout to lessen any chances of frightening it by dropping the line too close to it. I find it pays to make a short cast first and lengthen the line gradually until the drift is covering the lie.

If the trout ignores the fly but carries on feeding keep it up until the fish either accepts it or inspects it and turns away. While this may be frustrating you can take a certain measure of comfort from it. At least your casting hasn't put the trout down, so you're progressing in the right direction.

What fly should you be using? There is no substitute for hard experience here. If you have

Those hard-to-get-at places
Beyond the willow tree is a favourite trout lie. It requires delicacy and skill to flick your fly into such shady places.

learned to recognise the upwinged mayflies then you should try one of the upwinged patterns such as the Red Quill, Dad's Favourite, Greenwell's Glory or Twilight Beauty. Often the hook size is more important than the actual fly used. If the mayflies on the water are large then you may get away with a size 10 or 12 but the chances are you will be more successful using a 14 or even 16. Smaller than that is getting really tiny but you may find times when they will only look at size 18s or even smaller. Taken all round the size 14 is pretty standard.

If beetles are on the water you can use big bulky flies. The same applies when grasshoppers and cicadas are abundant during summer. With these bigger flies you can actually let them hit the water with a splash to draw a trout's attention to them. Unlike the fragile mayfly these large insects just don't land on the water gracefully.

There is one thing a dry-fly fisherman must learn and that is to avoid drag. Differing current speeds across the pool will cause loops and bellies to form in the line causing the fly to skitter across the surface. These bellies must be counteracted by carefully rolling them in the opposite direction.

This is known as mending a cast.

The exception is when caddis flies are hatching and scurrying across the surface of the pool. Trout will then take a dragged fly but all other times they will avoid it like the plague.

Now let us suppose one of your casts has been successful. You may have drifted your fly over a fish a dozen times without any response but suddenly there is a swirl and your fly is gone. It comes as a pleasant shock and the natural reflex is to lift the rod to strike. Your fly shoots out of the water without any resistance and tangles in the grass behind you. You have just committed the mistake we all have made at some time or other. With most types of fly fishing you can't strike quickly enough but different rules apply in this case. From the moment the trout's nose breaks the surface of the water, to the time it opens its mouth, inhales a quantity of water including your fly, and turns down again, a couple of seconds will have elapsed and it pays to give the fish another second for good grace before any attempt is made to pull the hook home. Do this and you'll find you will be successful.

Dry-fly fishing is great fun. You see the action

on the water's surface and this is its main appeal. It calls for a degree of casting proficiency but once that is mastered it becomes fairly easy. Some fly fishers become so wrapped up in it that they give up all other forms considering it to be the ultimate method of fly fishing. A good knowledge of basic streamside entymology helps and, if possible, the ability to tie small delicate flies. It you take up dry-fly fishing you will have embarked upon a lifetime apprenticeship.

Lake fishing

Still water presents its own difficulties. On all the lakes I have fished, excepting stream mouths, the best fishing is always associated with weed beds. The insect life is much greater in the proximity of a weedy bottom than it is over one of fine clean sand. Weed beds pose problems, especially if you are restricted to wading the shore. The best place to fish your fly is on the outside of weed beds and provided they don't reach too far out into the lake you can usually fish over them using a floating line and allowing the fly to sink deeply on a long leader, one of three metres or so. But if you have a boat you can anchor behind a weed bed and fish

Stillwater nymph fishing
Two fine brown trout taken by stillwater nymphing. The trout were feeding on hatching damsel and dragon nymphs in Lake Otamangakau, in the central North Island of New Zealand. Angler, Ron Burgin of Wairakei.

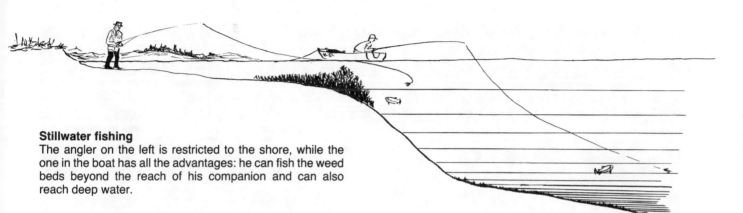

Stillwater fishing
The angler on the left is restricted to the shore, while the one in the boat has all the advantages: he can fish the weed beds beyond the reach of his companion and can also reach deep water.

over the edge. If the weed bed stretches far out into the lake, beyond the reach of the wader, you can just move your boat into position.

And of course you have the advantage if the trout are down deep in the holes of the lake. You put on a sinking line and fish anywhere you want to.

The fly fisherman who spends a lot of time stillwater fishing is best equipped with a boat. Next best, if the water is small and not subject to squalls, is a float tube (see p. 87).

The strike and playing the trout
Pat Barnes runs a tackle store in the township of West Yellowstone in the State of Montana, where he is known far and wide as an angler of considerable repute with a lifetime of sporting experience. Pat was helping me run a school for beginners and I was explaining the strike process.

"Keith", he interupted, "You strike a marlin but you don't strike trout — you merely tighten on them; the hook does the rest."

Early morning line-up
The mist of dawn clears to reveal a group of early-morning anglers at the mouth of the Te Wairoa stream, Lake Tarawera. They are fishing with lures and sinking lines, trying to tempt some of the monster trout for which the lake is famous.

I guess it's all a matter of definition and interpretation. The truth is I have seen some trout fishermen who do strike trout with a fair amount of muscle but Pat was correct and the term "tighten" better defines what should happen after a trout has taken your fly. You must pull down with your left hand on the line to draw in any slack and smartly lift your rod at the same time. The difference between a "strike" and a "tighten" depends on the type of gear being used and the methods. A strike on light dry-fly gear with a fine leader would probably result in a break-off while anything less than a hefty pull on 30 m of well-sunk fly line in a deep pool would probably be ineffectual.

"How will I know when a trout has taken my fly?" is a common question. In faster waters, when you're fishing wet flies or lures downstream, there is seldom any doubt. A quick snatch, a screaming reel and a leaping trout is pretty conclusive evidence that something has happened. However, sometimes the fly will just stop during the swing, just as though it has hooked up on the bottom. Then you will be surprised to find that when you

pull on the line to free it something pulls back. Sometimes when a trout is hooked it will dash straight towards you. If it leaps as it goes, this is very disconcerting for a beginner: you must use your left hand to pull in all the slack line as quickly as you can to keep the pressure on the fish. This is called stripping and the slack is dropped into the water until the fish turns direction and it can be allowed to run out again. Just keep a weather eye open and pray it doesn't tangle around your legs or an underwater stake that you missed seeing.

Never clamp down on a fish. You might pull the hook out. Let it have its head in the initial stages. The more it dashes around the sooner it will tire. Only put pressure on if absolutely necessary — such as when it seems the fish is going into a pile of snags or is about to head off into impassable water. Keep the rod tip up and allow the spring of the rod to absorb any sudden jerk or pull. Drop the rod tip down when the fish rushes off or leaps. Gradually an even pressure will tire the trout and it will allow itself to be drawn over the net or slid on to a beach.

9. Fly fishing from a boat

Fly fishing is usually associated with running streams but lakes, reservoirs and ponds can provide excellent stillwater fly fishing.

You can seek out a deep-water drop-off along a lake edge and search the depths with a sinking line and a large wet fly. Or you may use a floating line and a long leader to cast a nymph out past the weed beds where your slowly twitched offering may catch the attention of a speckled prowler finning its way along the edge of its weedy patrol. Or when a fall of insects is upon the lake's surface you may float a dry fly with every hope of success.

Some of these spots may be easily covered by wading the shoreline or casting dry-shod from rock ledges on outcrops, but a boat greatly increases your possibilities. You may anchor and search out drop-offs far beyond the reach of the shorebound angler, or you may use the boat to position yourself just back behind the edge of a pocket in the weed beds and prospect the edge of

the growths, or you may wish to fish along a cliff edge which would otherwise be inaccessible.

A light breeze can be used to allow the boat to drift slowly across the lake while you ply your fly, and once you've found an area that produces you can anchor the boat and begin casting in earnest.

A recent development over the last decade has been the proliferation of float tubes. These consist of a canvas seat and bib arrangement suspended in a large rubber tyre tube. The angler wears flippers to propel the tube backwards at about 2 knots maximum speed. This way the angler can cover weed beds and pockets or stalk rising fish. A word of caution however: these float tubes should never be used on running streams or large open waters.

There have been many cases of anglers using them on rivers and being washed under trees and banks or being capsized — with fatal results. Likewise on lakes if you get blown across to the opposite shore it should be always possible to walk back to your launching place so their use on wide open waters is strongly cautioned against.

So if you get the chance try a float. It's a branch of fly fishing which has much to offer, and used with care and caution the float tube is a great angler's aid. But if you have the choice, use a boat. It's safer and more comfortable.

The float tube
A comparatively new arrival on the angling scene, the float tube enables an angler to paddle out from the margins of a lake and fish the drop-offs and holes among the weed beds.

10. After dark

Some of the largest trout are caught during the night. Fish feed just as much in the dark as they do during daylight and lose a lot of their caution.

Good places are where streams run into lakes or where a tributary joins a big river. The tails of river pools also fish well after dark. The problem is that some anglers just don't like fishing after the sun has gone down. Besides having trouble with their casting and handling their gear, they become disorientated in the darkness.

Others take to it readily and as with all forms of fishing it's mainly a matter of practice. Once you can cast reasonably well and you've learned to retrieve line, you readily adapt.

Of course there are hazards associated with this form of fishing. One needs to be pretty familiar with the water to be fished for reasons of safety. Level sandy bottoms are to be preferred if wading. The mouths of small streams entering a lake usually provide safe footage.

You can catch trout on large streamer flies but even dry flies and nymphs will catch trout once the daylight has gone. It's a very productive time. Regulations vary from place to place. One district may allow fishing right round the clock — others will have a statutory finishing and beginning time. In some parts of the angling world night fishing for trout is prohibited. But if your district permits it, give it a try — if it appeals you will have discovered a very exciting time to fish.

The only addition required to normal gear is a small but dependable source of light. Some wear a flashlight hung around their neck — others like the flexilamp style of illumination which clips into the pocket of your vest or jacket and may be bent to direct the light beam to where the angler wants it — such as when tying on a new fly or landing a trout. Dress to insulate against the cool of the night and use stouter leaders as you may hook the trout of your dreams.

Night fishing
Fly fishing after dark has its rewards. It also pays the serious angler to carry a fish box in the car, as here. Made of metal or plastic, such a box keeps the car's interior free from slime and fishy smells.

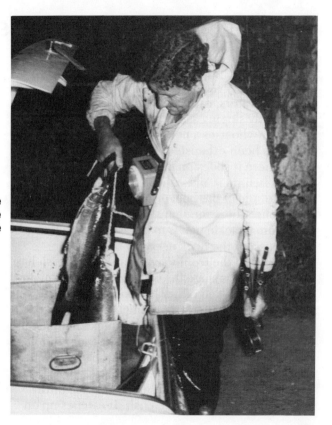

11. Netting or beaching a fish

On some waters, especially those having banks with gently sloping sandy edges, it is rare to meet an angler who uses a net. It is possible, after a trout has been exhausted, to lead it gently to the edge where it slides on its side. You then move quickly behind it and either move it up the beach with the side of the boot or use your hands to accomplish the same thing.

Terminal tackle needs to be reasonably strong to do this and the hook needs to be firmly embedded in the trout's jaw. Many a good fish has been lost at this stage through the angler using too much pressure and either breaking a fine and perhaps worn leader, or pulling the hook out. If this happens to you and you are quick enough you may be able to prevent the trout's escape, but if the fish is still fairly active it will probably flap its way back to freedom.

A landing net is nothing but a nuisance until you actually need it to net a fish. It catches up on bushes and brambles and is always in the way of whatever you are doing.

A folding net is an advantage, especially if carried in a belt pouch, but even then it catches up whenever you are scrambling down a bank or over a fence. However, on some streams, especially those with overgrown banks and cressy margins, a net is indispensable — especially if you want to release your catch unharmed.

Netting a trout in a fast stream is not an easy task. If a quiet side water can be found to manoeuvre the trout into, the problem is made a lot easier but where the water rushes along in tumbling haste a played-out trout of good weight imposes a great strain on tackle. Hold the trout up on the surface of the water, bring the net from behind and lower the rod tip to allow the fish to wash back into the net with the current. At the same time bring the net smartly forward and lift.

In all other circumstances where the current is

moderate or the water still, lead the trout into the net head first, lift the net smartly and drop the rod tip.

All the words in the world aren't going to make the netting of your first trout caught in a fast stream any easier. Of course small fish don't present much of a problem but the larger ones are difficult to manage. It often pays to lead your fish downstream until a quieter stretch of water is found.

If your leader is fine and the fly small, it can be a nerve-wracking time but this of course is part of the charm of fly fishing. It is a mixture of rewards and disappointments. That is what makes it so much of a challenge.

When selecting a landing net there are a few things to take into consideration. Make sure the net is big enough. The frame needs to accommodate easily the trout of the size you are likely to catch. Some streams have smaller trout than others where a smaller net would be of no great disadvantage but where you are liable to catch trout in excess of 2 kg (4½ lbs) the frame of the net needs to be large enough to accept a fish of that size and needs the net bag to be deep

enough so that the fish is fully trapped when the net is lifted from the water. Avoid nets with yellow or brightly coloured meshes. Green is by far the best colour as it seems that the trout sometimes think it is weed and will swim into it quite calmly whereas a yellow net causes them to struggle and try to turn away from it.

At all times use the net with stealth. The only time it is handled with speed is when the lift is made. Slip the net into the water slowly, make sure the bag is not tangled and then lead the fish gently into it — head first. Once half the fish's length is over the frame lift quickly and it's yours. If the trout struggles too much drop the rod tip and let it swim off then, applying gentle pressure again, make another attempt. If the trout is still strong postpone the netting until the fish is easier to manage.

It is my experience that a fish takes a much shorter time to land with a net than it does to beach. With experience a fish can be netted fairly easily if it is done with care, but it needs to be thoroughly played out before it will allow itself to be beached.

Always wash your net after use and remove the

slime. Mice like gnawing through the meshes of nets which have dried with fish slime on them and many an angler has found great holes in the landing net when it has not been washed clean and hung up in the shed for the little rodents' delight.

Choose a net with a nylon mesh. Cotton rots and it's not funny to have a large trout break through the net back into the water. If you choose a folding net be certain it's not the type that collapses when you lift a fish with it. The better types all have a catch to lock the arms in an extended position when in use. A spring-loaded release enables the arms to be folded back against the handle so that it can be carried in the collapsed position. Some nets are available with telescopic handles — a definite advantage when landing a fish from a bank or reaching over weed beds, but if you buy such a net make certain it has a positive locking system. Some nets with telescopic sections have a habit of turning when a fish is lifted — sometimes with dire consequences.

I have three landing nets, one a collapsible belt net which I use on smaller bush-hemmed streams, a fixed net with large frame and 70 cm handle which I use when fishing from a boat and a similar net with a long handle which doubles as a wading staff when I'm fishing some of the bigger, more boisterous rivers.

To sum it all up, you will land more fish in the long run if you use a net but you have to be prepared to put up with the inconvenience it is going to cause you.

Of course you may gill a fish with your hands but this should only be done if you are going to kill the fish, as it is badly damaged in the process.

Gilling a fish is an art, and the success of it is based on a fine sense of timing.

Occasionally one will hook a trout in circumstances where the net has not been brought along and there are no suitable places to beach it. Sometimes it can be slid into a crevice between the boulders but on occasions even this isn't possible. Once a trout has been played out completely it can be led against a rock or if you are wading it can be coaxed close in by your leg.

The right hand (or left if you're left-handed) with thumb extended is brought down over the top of the fish's gills and the fish is suddenly grasped with such force that the gill covers of the fish are collapsed. This paralyses the fish and it is easily lifted from the water. There is no room for indecision — if the fish is brushed by your fingers or your grip isn't strong enough, the fish will either dash off again or flap itself free. Once a person has completed this operation successfully there is no problem with it again. But remember — use your thumb and fingers with speed and sufficient force to make them a set of powerful pincers.

If a fish is being returned alive to the water, remove the hook with care and handle the fish as little as possible. The slime on a fish is its protective coating preventing fungi growth and diseases from infecting its skin. Some schools of thought advocate wetting your hand before touching them — others say a dry hand is best. Another opinion is that the heat of our hand causes a fish's skin to scald so no matter what method you use be careful. If you are using a net the hook may be removed while the trout is held in the water. A pair of angler's forceps helps in removing the hook and the fish may be released with little or no damage.

Gilling a trout
The young angler has beached his trout in the shallows at his feet. Then quickly reaching down he has gilled it out of the water.

Most anglers have had the experience of releasing a trout and catching it again shortly afterwards so if care is taken it seems that no lasting effects are felt by the trout. Make sure an exhausted fish is held in the current facing upstream until its gills are working properly and it is able to swim away under its own power. I am appalled when I see anglers return fish with underarm lobs regardless of the safety of the trout. They are a valuable commodity — return with care those you don't wish to kill.

Without a net
The author prepares to gill a fish after playing it to a standstill. It is lifted to the surface and seized firmly across the back of the head.

12. Wading

To some, wading is a dangerous exercise to be avoided if at all possible. To others it is an adventurous challenge and they slosh into the water without regard for safety and often to the detriment of their angling success.

The prudent angler wades only when necessary. You should do so either to cross a river or stream, or in order to place a cast into water you would not otherwise be able to reach.

Some anglers become giddy and disorientated if they are standing in swiftly moving water. If this is a problem they are unable to overcome, they are best advised to stay out of fast water. The more gentle currents are for them. If you find yourself in a situation where the current causes you to feel as though you are losing your balance, then you should look straight ahead at the trees or opposite bank until the feeling has passed, then move with caution back to safer bottom.

River crossings — except in slow or very shallow places — are usually made on a downstream diagonal. Shallower bars in a river or stream always follow that pattern and since it means going down with the current slightly it is made easier. However the same crossing in reverse means pushing up against the current and if the original crossing was difficult the return may well be almost impossible. A great aid in such places is a wading staff. It may be a branch picked up from among a pile of driftwood or cut from a standing sapling. Some anglers carry a staff of aluminium with a spiked point and a rubber handgrip. With a staff one can lean into the current by placing it upstream and then moving the feet cautiously one at a time. Never move a foot unless the other is firmly placed on the bottom.

Beware of deep channels against the far bank. Many an angler has spent anxious minutes picking his way through a dubious crossing only to find the last short section to the safety of the bank is made impossible by a deep run under the bank or close by the far edge.

Choose your crossings with care and if at all uncertain — don't try it. Rubber-soled waders can be dangerous. In bouldery rivers they are a positive menace and tend to slip very easily. Cleated heel plates help to obtain a better grip but by far the safest waders have felt soles. Unless you've worn felt-soled waders you just cannot believe how much easier wading becomes. One can move with confidence. It isn't just falling in and drowning which needs to be avoided. Many anglers have suffered injury and bruising through slipping over in only a few inches of bouldery water because the rubber soles of their waders turned the river-bed stones into greasy cannonballs.

The choice between hip boots or chest waders depends entirely on the water to be fished. Small streams can be easily crossed wearing the shorter waders while the larger pools of some of the bigger rivers dictate that chest waders are imperative if the angler is to cast a fly to the deeper run under the far bank. It also depends on whether the angler has far to walk between fishing spots. My choice is for chest waders in the long run. If it's summertime I prefer to wear a pair of wading boots and shorts but our Australian cousins wouldn't wear shorts along some of their stream banks during the snake season. So the type of wader used depends on the size of the water, the climate and other factors as well as your individual preference.

The possibility of drowning is always closely associated with wading and of course it shouldn't be taken too lightly. I have been swept off my feet on three occasions and emerged each time unscathed. I swam out. Writers of thrillers and others maintain that if you tip in while wearing chest waders the air trapped in the boots causes your feet to pop to the top while you are suspended upside down in the water. This is contrary to my experience.

The pressure of water on the legs forces all the air out of the feet and legs. The air trapped around the chest and shoulders, especially if you are wearing a waterproof parka, helps to suspend you in the water — provided you don't panic. I know this is easy to say when sitting on dry land but if you can swim you need have no great fear under normal circumstances. If the current washes you down tumbling rapids or against a cliff you're in serious trouble but in normal pools it's possible to swim out to the edge. That's when the fun begins because you have to crawl out. I'm not advocating going for swims in fast rivers wearing chest waders but it doesn't mean automatic drowning if you do go in.

It does pay to wear a safety vest. Some are available with built-in buoyancy pads, while others have inflatable life preservers built into them which may be mouth inflated if an angler feels he's entering an uncertain situation, or, inflated in an emergency by pulling a rip cord which releases a compressed air cylinder. The last is perhaps the safest of all safeguards, except staying away from the water altogether — and anyone with that outlook wouldn't be reading this book!

For fishing larger waters chest waders are desirable but for fishing smaller streams hip boots are adequate.

13. Aids and accessories

If you become an avid fly angler you can bury yourself under a literal mountain of aids and accessories. You may carry a small book for identifying insects and phials of preserving fluid for collecting specimens. You may carry a magnifying glass to assist in their identification. You may well carry a thermometer to check on water temperatures. You may have a little gadget to assist in tying difficult knots and even another magnifying glass to help tie on a fresh fly. You will probably have a pair of scissors or clippers with which to cut nylon. You're bound to have several spools of nylon of varying diameters and breaking strains as well as several cards of one-piece tapered leaders. You will have a bottle of dry-fly flotant and another of a preparation to make things sink (sometimes with the labels worn off so that you aren't sure which is which). You may have a leader gauge to check the diameter of your nylon because you never believe the manufacturer's calibrations.

You will have a box full of large wet flies and streamers, another box full of dry flies of varying patterns, and yet another box will contain hordes of nymph patterns covering the largest dragonfly larvae through various mayfly nymphs down to the smallest midge larva imaginable. You will have a pair of polaroid glasses to spot fish through the otherwise impenetrable surface glare of the water — plus your own spectacles to assist you with the difficult job of going through all this paraphernalia when you're in search of something you can't find! Then you may have a parcel of sandwiches, an apple and/or an orange, a spare spool of lead wire, a tin with spare rod guides and tape, a container of split shot to sink your flies in those deepest of runs (if the local rules allow it), a plastic envelope of stick-on indicators for nymph fishing, a needle to assist in tying nail knots and a knife that doubles for cleaning fish and being used

as a balance for weighing them after capture. And
of course there is a light waterproof coat in case
the weather turns on its worst and a plastic bag to
wrap the fish in.

And where is all this impedimenta stored?
Why, in an angling vest! The aforegoing is a pretty
good description of most anglers' vests, and while
I must admit that I need a reference file to locate a
required article in mine it is without doubt an
almost indispensable part of my fishing tackle.
The pockets allow for an even distribution of fly
boxes, etc., while the back pouch is ideal for
carrying the odd fish and a raincoat.

The alternative is a bag. If I am on a long day's
fishing with a fair amount of walking involved I
use a rucksack. It sits better on the shoulders and

Angling vests

Christine and Michael Fong, well-known American photo-
graphic and writing duo, illustrate the modern complete
angler. Their vests have pockets to accommodate all their
angling knick-knacks. Eyeshades keep the sun off their
faces and the polarised glasses, which block out glare
reflected off the surface of the water, are an essential part
of the equipment.

carries the few extra items I'm likely to need for a long day on the water. It also means I stow my waders in it and wear a pair of light boots when hiking up the river bank or across the hills to reach the water I'm going to fish.

A shoulder bag is fine so long as you are only carrying a few bits and pieces with you. Anything over a kilo or two and the single strap makes the shoulder sore.

One type of canvas bag which is becoming popular is the "Arctic Creel" style of bag which is dipped regularly into the water. The evaporation from the canvas keeps the contents cool. I have no personal experience of these but American friends assure me they do a great job during a long hot summer's day.

For extended fishing trips a rucksack may be preferred, but this angler finds a shoulder bag adequate for carrying his few bits and pieces.

14. Handling the catch

Having landed your trout you must decide what to do with it. If you wish to return it to the water, so it may live to fight another day, do so quickly and with a minimum of handling. Remove the hook as soon as possible and hold the trout facing into the current. Its gills will begin to open and close and as it regains its senses it will give a quick wriggle and dart off into the river. You should always keep your hands wet when handling fish to cause a minimum of damage. It is also believed that a dry human hand actually causes scalds on the trout's skin, which is used to much lower temperatures than human blood heat.

If you intend to keep the fish, you should firstly ascertain that it is of legal keeping length. If it's above the minimum size it should be dispatched with a sharp blow on the head. A piece of stick, a stone or a "priest" should be used. I use the back of a folding knife I carry in my vest.

After killing the trout the best thing to do next is to clean it. If you wish to leave the head on, be sure to remove the gills. Take out the stomach and be sure to remove the black strip along the backbone. This is the trout's kidney and if left in it will cause the flesh to spoil. Dry the trout with grass, willow leaves or paper and place the fish in your bag. It pays to have a plastic bag to stop the slime getting on to the canvas. Bury the offal from the trout away from the riverside. In some districts this is law.

If you are going to spend all day fishing don't carry the trout in your bag unless you have to. Hang any fish in the shade of a tree. Put a small stick in the stomach cavity to keep it open and it'll dry out quickly. Be sure the shade isn't going to shift away in an hour or so; choose your spot with care. If the trout are dry the flies won't bother them.

Of course the best thing to do is to get them into a refrigerator as soon as possible.

When it comes to cooking your catch consult a cooking book. *The New Zealand Trout Cookbook* by Carole Condé-Acheson, published by my own publishers, is now in the book shops and is full of delightful recipes. Many people complain that trout are full of bones so they don't like eating them. Of course they are full of bones, so were the snapper and whiting that they bought from the fish shops before the fishmonger filleted them! The answer is to fillet the trout and remove the bones and skin.

To do this properly you need a fish filleting knife with a slender flexible blade. This is essential as other types of knives only make the job difficult and leave more flesh on the skeleton than they do on the fillet.

Begin by running the knife from the head along the side of the backbone. A sharp knife slides along the ribs, and you will feel it slicing through the thin lateral bones, which are only found along the front half of the fillet. These can be removed later.

After both sides have been filleted, lay them with the skin side down. Rub your fingers over the fillet and you will feel the ends of the lateral bones. You can pull them out with pliers if you wish, or remove them by making a cut on each side and removing the strip of flesh complete with bones.

To skin the fillet you need a board about 2 cm thick. Cut the skin back from the tail end of the fillet. Make sure the skin is downside then just saw the knife between the flesh and skin pulling on the tail end of the skin. If the knife is sharp and the fish is fresh, fillet and skin will separate beautifully.

That's all there is to it and you have completely boneless trout. So go to it — turn the rewards of your day on the lake or stream into a mouth-watering dish.

Conclusion

In the preceding chapters I have tried to explain in what I hope are simple terms just exactly what fly fishing is all about. If it has assisted the reader in steering him or her towards the enjoyment of a wonderful sport I will have succeeded.

But a book of this sort is nothing more than a crutch; if you are a beginner you will have to go out and go through all the trials and errors the rest of us have had to go through. I hope this book will help you to recognise and correct those mistakes. You can only go so far by yourself. To increase your enjoyment and knowledge you should join an angling club. You should join a conservation movement dedicated to preserving pure clean waters and a healthy environment — for by doing this you are helping to protect nature and its creatures — including of course ourselves.

Make yourself aware of the rules and regulations governing your sport. These vary from district to district and from country to country, but all regulations are in force for the greater protection and utilisation of the sport of fly fishing. We should try not to be selfish in our angling pursuits, and should treat others as we would have them treat us.

A beautiful trout stream to oneself is every angler's dream, but in these days of waterway alienation for the increasing demands of development a lone angler defending his stream against politicians and engineers hasn't a chance. The more people who enjoy the rapture of tumbling waters, the long lithe rod and the graceful roll of a swishing line, the better our chances to preserve the wild trout waters which mean so much to us who really care.

And, oh yes! Do watch that back cast, won't you? Good luck.

The author

Keith Draper is the best-known fishing personality in a country famous for its trout angling. He was born in Hawke's Bay, but now lives by the shore of Lake Taupo, where he runs a fly-tying and fishing-tackle wholesale business. He has been a professional fishing guide and instructor, and is the author of *Angling in New Zealand*, *Tie a Fly*, *Nymphs for all Seasons* and the definitive *Trout Flies in New Zealand*.

He is seen here with a brown trout caught on a Hare and Copper nymph as it cruised among the weed beds of Lake Otamangakau.